Let these words do
the good work they can.

God is a poet, and so is Laura Wifler. With theological steadiness and lyrical beauty, Laura's words remind us that poetry speaks most profoundly when it is anchored in what is true. Her poems do not merely move us; they disciple us into confession, worship, hope, and the interplay between the mundane and the transcendent that we so often miss. In a world parched for poetry, here is water for the thirsty.

JEN WILKIN
Author and Bible teacher

This Side of the Sky will both upend your expectations and mend your weary heart with gospel hope. Laura's poetry startles the slumbering soul awake. Her poignant words offer a glass of cold lemonade on a sweltering summer day and a warm blanket to wrap up in when life feels too fragile to hold your ache. More than poetry or prose, this book is a beautiful weaving of longing, lament, and praise. Laura invites you to pull up a chair, pour a cup of coffee, and as she says, "unbutton your heart" to the faithful, freeing life before you—this side of the sky.

GRETCHEN SAFFLES
Bestselling author of *The Well-Watered Woman* and *Word Before World*

No writer describes the feeling of motherhood and the unbearable joy and grief of change as our children grow up the way Laura Wifler does. I closed this book feeling understood, as if she spoke for me too.

ERIN NAPIER
Star of HGTV's *Home Town* and *New York Times* bestselling author of *Heirloom Rooms* and *The Lantern House*

Poetry is paying attention to the griefs, glories, grit, and gifts of this beautiful, broken world. In this collection, Laura helps us do just that: pay attention. Few things are harder to do; few things more important to practice.

KYLE WORLEY
Pastor and author of *Home with God: Our Union with Christ*

I came to poetry later in my life because, in all honesty, I was intimidated by it. Then I met Robert Frost as he told me about "Stopping by Woods on a Snowing Evening," and something unlocked that gave me an insatiable appetite for the economy of words that could unpack such a vast expression of meaning. In my search for more, I discovered lots of wonderful poetry on social media—of all places—and I found myself following poets I wanted to read more from. That's how I found Laura Wifler's poetry, and I am thrilled for this collection in book form. Read it not just for the insightful poetry she offers but for the familiarity her words will cultivate in you for the larger, necessary world of poetry itself.

RUSS RAMSEY
Author of *Van Gogh Has a Broken Heart: What Art Teaches Us About the Wonder and Struggle of Being Alive*

Reading *This Side of the Sky* feels like a pause with a dear friend. It's a hug, a reset in the middle of a chaotic day, a deeply needed sigh. The short reflections carry weighty truth, reaching straight to the soul, like marrow to the bones you didn't realize were aching. And you know it's a wonderful read when you're sad it's over.

GWEN HEFNER
The Makerista

Laura is a noticer and a wonderer, and her poems invite us into that same sacred attentiveness. *This Side of the Sky* awakens us to God's presence in the present moment, even when our lives feel small or ordinary. The poems on these pages help us name both the ache and the joy of being human as we move through life's winding seasons. In a weary world that often prizes tidy answers over honest connection and reflection, I'm so grateful for faithful art like this—words rooted in tenderness and anchored in Christ-centered hope.

KAYLA CRAIG
Author of *Our Daily Breath*, *To Light Their Way*, and *Every Season Sacred*; creator of Liturgies for Parents

THIS SIDE OF THE SKY

101 POEMS AND SCRIPTURES
FOR THE HUNGRY, HOPEFUL, AND HOMESICK

LAURA WIFLER

TYNDALE
MOMENTUM™

A Tyndale nonfiction imprint

Visit Tyndale online at tyndale.com.

Visit Tyndale Momentum online at tyndalemomentum.com.

Visit the author online at laurawifler.com.

This Side of the Sky: 101 Poems and Scriptures for the Hungry, Hopeful, and Homesick

Jacket photograph of cloud study by Frederic Edwin Church on Rawpixel, public domain.

Cover, jacket, and interior photograph of black and white clouds by Joseph August Knip on Rawpixel, public domain.

Designed by Libby Dykstra

Edited by Stephanie Rische

Author is represented by Jenni Burke of Illuminate Literary Agency: illuminateliterary.com.

For information about special discounts for bulk purchases, please contact Tyndale House Publishers at csresponse@tyndale.com, or call 1-855-277-9400.

Library of Congress Cataloging-in-Publication Data

A catalog record for this book is available from the Library of Congress.

ISBN 979-8-4005-1605-4

Printed in China

32 31 30 29 28 27 26
7 6 5 4 3 2 1

For the ones who watch the skies.

Remember: He is here with you,
on this side of the sky, working
and moving through His Spirit.
Yet someday—if He does not
call you home first—you'll see
the sky collapse like a star, like
a lung, as Heaven and Earth
collide in one consummate gasp.

For now, you remain.

It should not stop you, though,
from rubbing your rib cage with
want and tracking the clouds for
His return.

What they say really is true:
Today, anything can happen.

CONTENTS

LET THESE WORDS DO THE GOOD WORK THEY CAN

I am so coarse, the things the poets see
Are obstinately invisible to me.
C. S. LEWIS, "A CONFESSION"

FOR MOST OF MY LIFE, I believed I was too obtuse to understand poetry. I was a student of English and journalism in college, so it wasn't that I didn't try. Book after book stumbled onto my nightstand, both required reading and random library pickups, as I tried desperately to love it. I wanted to cradle a word, to feel time suspend while I chewed on a turn of phrase, to sigh after I clearly understood what meaning lay beyond a line.

But I never could. It wasn't that I didn't love it. It was that I didn't even like it. I swore off poetry the same way I did glitter craft projects in the house, hanging my own wallpaper, or drinking oat milk. Poetry wasn't for me.

Until the year—the one and only year—I homeschooled my two oldest children. That spring, the world went fragile and everyone was baking sourdough in sweatpants and opening neighborhood barber shops on their back decks. Normal life was a distant fog, and being in our own four walls for months on end made us all a little weird. But also a little bit brave. Including me.

Our homeschooling curriculum included a unit on poetry. My kids and I read selected passages aloud together, and we chose several of our favorites to memorize. Contrary to every experience I'd had with poetry in the past, I loved it. These poems were straightforward but resonant, like a lemon cake or my favorite red lipstick. They said something in a way I could easily understand while being beautiful enough that I never wanted to forget.

Eventually, the curriculum had my children writing their own poetry, so I gathered my courage and started writing with them. Almost at once, I felt like I had come home. I was spellbound by the practice, finally alive in my writing. As silly as it sounds, through a unit designed for kindergartners and second graders, I learned that I had a lot of misconceptions about poetry. It doesn't have to rhyme or follow a strict pattern of syllables or be laid out in a specific meter or be hard to understand.

And perhaps my biggest lightbulb: Poetry has no true rules.

After that year, homeschooling didn't stick, but poetry did. As someone who had been freely offering her writing on the internet for more than 12 years, I unabashedly started to share some of my work online. I preferred to label it "emotive microblogs," still groping for the confidence to label my poetry what it was and scared that I might just like—and now be writing—poetry.

But readers could tell. Previously, most of my writing centered on nonfiction pieces, through microblogs, essays, articles, and traditional books. But as my writing changed, my readers left notes using the *p*-word.

"Thanks for this poem!"

"I shared this poem with my friend."

I was surprised by their declarations. It was lyrical! Heartfelt! Not actually poetry. I claimed it was just "tiny musical musings." Joke's on me—because being "musical" is exactly one of the defining traits of poetry. But eventually, the term stacked up often enough from my readers that I had to admit I had become the very thing I thought wasn't for me: I was a poet.

Over the years, I've heard hundreds of stories about people's perceptions of poetry. Some love it. They regularly savor it, discuss it, and share it. Others, like the old me, feel that poetry is confusing, intimidating, or reserved for someone else—someone more intellectual or sophisticated. And some have never really given it much thought. It's a literary category they're not into, and that's about it.

No matter where you're coming from with poetry, I'm so thankful you've opened this book.

Since poetry can be such a polarizing genre, I wanted to offer a few thoughts as you read. One of the biggest rules of poetry is that there are no rules, but I think it can help to engage with this art form by bearing a few things in mind and allowing poetry to do its best work in our hearts.

First, know that the poems and meditations included in this book are wide and varied. The thread that strings them together is the subject of my life, I suppose. A woman in her late thirties, living in rural America with her husband, three kids, and one adorable goldendoodle. I shared the joys and griefs I could, but there are many more that shape my story, ones I cannot or will not share publicly in a book. Ultimately, know that these are the poems and meditations of a woman, probably very much like you, searching for hope and meaning in a life that, while it has many glimmers of beauty, is also often filled with confusion, difficulty, and pain. It is a life that is good, but also hard.

Now, I realize this sounds obvious, but when reading, remember that you and I are not exactly the same. I am married. You might not be. I have a child with intellectual disabilities. It's possible you've never had a close relationship with someone who has a significant disability. And that's okay. But know that I have not nuanced my writing to acknowledge every situation (as is common in nonfiction writing); instead, I am trusting you, dear reader, to find something of value even if the particulars of our two lives don't align. Our specific joys, sufferings, celebrations, and griefs might be different, but I have come to find these experiences share a pulse and you may find the rhythm familiar, if you have ears to hear.

Take what you need and leave the rest.

Second, I write from the perspective of a Christian. This means that I believe God made the world and everything in it. He made man and woman in His image, yet they rebelled in the garden, rejecting God's good plan for their lives. This severed humanity's relationship with God and brought sin and death into the world. But God, in His love, sent His Son, Jesus Christ, to willingly die in our place on the cross—yet He didn't stay dead. Jesus rose from the grave three days later, showing Himself to His disciples and hundreds of other witnesses. Then He ascended into Heaven and now sits at the right hand of God. But God didn't leave us here alone. Those who trust in Christ receive the Holy Spirit to help us walk in obedience to God's will and ways in this life. We also have the promise of a home in Heaven to look forward to, where there will be no more pain, no more sorrow, no more tears. It is there we will spend eternity with our God and Savior, forever.

I believe this down to my trembling bones. It is a truth and hope that leads my life like a beckoning hand and presses its thumb into every part of my being.

This means that all the writing you'll find here is informed and shaped by the gospel. In some of the poetry, you'll see that I have taken liberties to imagine the lifestyles and thoughts of biblical characters, as well as used metaphors and similes from Scripture and woven in common Christian colloquialisms to offer further meaning. I am not claiming to have additional revelations; I'm simply shading in the yearnings and contours of my art.

I've laid out the book in five acts, loosely following the typical Christian experience. If you appreciate a clear roadmap, here's where we're headed:

- **ACT 1:** ***Acknowledge the Ache***
  We realize this life is very hard, due to both our own sin and the brokenness of the world.
- **ACT II:** ***Listen for the Hymns of Promise***
  We see glimmers of what might be hope and healing for our pain.
- **ACT III:** ***Unbutton Your Heart***
  We lay down our cares and wrongdoings at the Savior's feet and receive salvation.
- **INTERMISSION:** ***A Moment to Address the Body in the Room***
  If you are a woman, this needs no explanation.
- **ACT IV:** ***Wear the Crown of Creation***
  We fight the good fight with Christ by our side.
- **ACT V:** ***Bury It in Your Bones***
  We cling to the hope of Heaven with a white-knuckle grip until this life takes us to the next.

Not every poem or meditation fits neatly into a category, but I've given careful consideration to the placement of each one. I've tied each entry to a Scripture excerpt to help ground it and offer more spiritual depth—but as I mentioned before, in the end, it's not about my particular meaning; it's about how the verses and entries speak to you and how God uses them in your life.

So once again, take what's helpful and leave the rest.

My prayer is that these poems rightly reckon with the realities of the world you and I live in while also testifying to a believer's divine home and the transcendent promises we have access to right now in Christ. This is what poetry, at its best, can do. It not only listens and names, but it also points us to the greater reality that sometimes feels just beyond reach. Like there is a veil or shroud, and for a moment, you see the edges flutter or a corner shimmer. Holy mystery haunts every surface of our lives, if we only know how to look.

As time has gone on, I've become more comfortable with the title *poet*. Though even now, it sometimes feels like it doesn't quite fit—like wearing a fancy dress on a night out. A bit formal and tight for a woman who prefers sneakers and ponytails, even if it matches the dress code.

I think what finally made me a believer was realizing that poetry isn't meant to be perfectly understood from every direction; it's simply meant to be received with a grace-filled heart. So come with your whole self. Aching. Soft. Open. Let these words do the good work they can. Let them pump you full.

The woman saw that the tree was good for food and delightful to look at, and that it was desirable for obtaining wisdom. So she took some of its fruit and ate it. GENESIS 3:6

Good

I want to know how Eve felt, knowing
nothing but the tending of light. I want to
know how it felt to be full and heavy
with good, pulsing with the strange
creature of perfection. I want to know
the unmarred pleasure of a day,
to have stood by the sea
next to the Word that formed it.

I want to know how Eve felt, grasping
Hope's hand. Maybe she got goosebumps.
Maybe she shivered. I want to know
how it felt to wake up under
the moon and look into Joy's
face. Love, I would guess,
is a pleasant companion.

I wonder if Eve's hand touched
a tree, a rock, a flower, to say, *Hello,*
it's nice to meet you. I wonder
if they leaned in to say hello back.

It's too bad, then, that Eve
felt it was too good to be true.

ACT I

ACKNOWLEDGE THE ACHE

The wide world is all about you: you can fence yourselves in, but you cannot forever fence it out.

J. R. R. TOLKIEN, *THE FELLOWSHIP OF THE RING*

NOTHING LASTS FOREVER. At least nothing of form and physicality. There's a concept in thermodynamics called *entropy*, which is the measure of disorder or chaos in a system. It captures the way that over time, without careful attention, governments bloat, your refrigerator moans and warms, and makeup tubes and hairbrushes stack up on your bathroom counter. Entropy wants to happen anywhere there is supposed to be structure, energy, or order, reminding us that without considerable effort, everything in the universe (from gardens to friendships to our galaxy) is naturally barreling toward decay and chaos.

If you have lived long enough, you don't need a scientist to label this for you. You sense entropy all around you. Life is hard, and it's only getting harder. Adam and Eve launched us into a post-fall world, and ever since, life has been riddled with pain, sorrow, and grief. This is due to both humanity's sin and the curse on the earth, causing endless toil, brokenness, and the now-diagnosed entropy.

In the wake of any grief, the first step toward healing is to acknowledge what happened. To be honest about the flat notes of this life and to listen fully to their deafening tone. It is owning that you are not perfect and there are many things you have done wrong—against others and against the God of the universe. It is also admitting that there are many ways people have wronged you. You have been treated unfairly, and that's not okay. And finally, it is recognizing the countless ways this world has gone sideways. The things that happen don't make sense—and they shouldn't! Because this is not the way this world was meant to be.

So acknowledge the ache of this life. Swallow, roll, rage, and roar. Feel fully the throb in your chest and the pounding in your heart. Wail, if you need to. This world has gone wild, and you with it. There will be time to sort it all out, but that time is not right now.

From the rising of the sun to its setting,
let the name of the LORD be praised. PSALM 113:3

Peel

Each morning I make yellow eggs for the kids
then wake them with back rubs
and don't stop the dog
from licking their cheeks.
I do hair, change diapers,
put shoes on feet.
I find drumsticks for band
and am a volunteer
for a "quick magic trick
I just made up."
(I act surprised.)
And this is only in the first
twenty minutes of a morning.
Each night I peel away
the day, sometimes crying
in the shower, sometimes
on the floor in prayer, sometimes
frenetic on the couch,
sometimes (most times)
memorizing the velvet curves
of the moon in the dark mouth
of the night before I slip
beneath the sheets.

He said to them all, "If anyone wants to follow after me, let him deny himself, take up his cross daily, and follow me." LUKE 9:23

Sometimes It Is the Littlest Things

1.

What I know is sometimes, it is the little things that are heaviest for me to carry for Christ. The big things—the disability, the chronic pain, the deaths, the family skeleton that walked out of the closet—I have a track record of handing them off to God the way a barista hands you coffee. I know where they go. Right there. No, no, a little to the left, so the shadow of the cross covers them in full.

2.

I want to blame the car seat, because it is always the car seat. I know this. I know it will never be welcome at 3 p.m., but as I tell her, it is required by law. This, for some reason, seems to make no difference to her. Most days I am patient. *How about a snack? How about a drink? I know it is hard, honey, I know it is awful, I know this is not the way you want to wake up.* But other days, I am short and cold, and I don't want to admit it but there, I said it.

3.

I stare at the fire and wonder how I would respond if someone said I must renounce Christ or they will give me a one-way ticket to Heaven.

4.
I disagree with the turn the conversation has taken in the group of women I am with. I share a different opinion. "Why?" they ask. "Science," I tell them. I do not mention the God-factor.

5.
I wonder if we all have it mixed up. We seek God when our mothers are sick and our headaches are chronic and when we need a job, a dollar, a cure. We put them all in a big basket and shove them across the table with one eye closed—*You take them God, You be sovereign, You do what You do.*

Do not hear me wrong, this is good and right.

But what about when you said, *Enough!* but you didn't say it like honey? What about when you felt like you should have hung back and talked to that person who usually goes unseen, but you shoved it down so you could talk to someone more fun? What about when you decided your perfectly good dishes are suddenly good for nothing, and yes they are only dishes but they are aiming an arrow straight at your covetous heart?

6.
What about the car seat? What about the science?

Sometimes it is the little things that are heaviest to carry for Christ.

Behold, children are a heritage from the LORD,
the fruit of the womb a reward. PSALM 127:3, ESV

Welcome Home

"Children may outgrow your lap, but they will never outgrow your heart." She smells of attic and malt, and smiles at her saying, thinking she is clever. I nod and smile back: "Good one, so true," I say. I wonder there in the grocery store, my cart askew and filled with curly pasta and oranges, if she knows that *atrium* is Latin for "entrance hall" or that *ventricle* means "womb." I wonder if she knows how each morning, when my children's fresh faces greet me, all I dream of is welcoming them through my beating heart's pulsing front door, counting their straight spines—

one, *two*, *three*, and ushering them *further! further!* away from this dark world until they are right back where they belong.

Pay careful attention, then, to how you walk—not as unwise people but as wise—making the most of the time. EPHESIANS 5:15-16

Urgent

They say by the time my child turns 12,
I will have spent 75 percent of my time with them.
I am sitting at the kitchen island and decide I will reject this.
My children will live with me forever, I think,
as any self-respecting mother would allow. I tell myself
we will be the exception. We will be the family that is together
until death. The thoughts hang like a shrunken blanket,
a comfort, but useless. Then—

I push off the counter stool, throat strangled, hands scrambling,
salt in my eyes. Gasping for hours, minutes, seconds
with their pure faces in front of mine, I rush
to find them. Here, one in the living room
reading by the fire. Here, one in the basement
playing with tiny, colorful animals. Here,
one in the garage searching for a football.

Look, our time with our children is so short
and urgent and ordinary. All we can do
is settle in the moment—to listen to
their stories on the driveway while
the cicadas hum and the crows sing.
Search for wild raspberries in the woods,
quiet with full mouths and reverence. Touch
each other's skin, hand to hand, cheek
to cheek. Sip lemonade and lick popsicles on the back porch
under the fading stars. I confess
I don't know how to let them go,
but each day, in life's mercifully slow way,
we discover them, limbs and hearts and minds.
All you can beg for is time.

Little children, let us not love in word or talk but in deed and in truth. 1 JOHN 3:18, ESV

You Might Be Surprised

In fifth grade, my friends and I were at the softball diamond during recess. They whispered behind their hands and I grinned like I was in on the secret, though I had no idea what they were talking about. "You do it. No, you do it! No, you!" They giggled. Finally a brave soul walked to me and said, "We don't want to be friends with you anymore. You can't hang out with us." I went to the merry-go-round, running, running, running, letting the wind take my tears.

//

A text arrives inviting my daughter with disabilities to a birthday party. A classmate from school. The party includes makeup and tea and they are to "wear something fancy." I read the text two times to be sure. My daughter has a friend who would like to have her at their birthday. I read it aloud to my husband. The lower half of my vision turns cloudy. "She'll be there!" I text. "I'll send an aide with her. She will love it!"

//

Sometimes I think about how everyone is sweet and kind to a child with disabilities but when that child is grown, people are uncomfortable, impatient, or a little bit afraid. I wonder how long people will be generous. Is that too honest? Is your heart breaking, like mine, even a little, because deep down you know this is true?

//

In high school I was not the popular one, I was the everyone's-friend one. It is because I was kind. I was kind because I knew what it felt like for people to be mean. I was kind because the Holy Spirit was doing supernatural things in my soul. I was kind because I knew my mother would have my head if I wasn't.

//

I am thinking about how we each must choose something, a few things, to give our life to and I cannot expect everyone's to be disability. I am thinking about how it is not really asking you to care about disability, it is asking you to care about people. I am thinking about how just yesterday, my son said in surprise, "I don't know why I am saying this but I am really glad we have disability in our family." I am thinking about how other people, if given the chance, might be surprised as well.

Everyone should look not to his own interests, but rather to the interests of others. PHILIPPIANS 2:4

The Vaults

Today I am visiting Edinburgh with my family, and we are nearly in tears with astonishment as we learn all that can happen on one piece of earth. We signed up to tour the Edinburgh Vaults, small rooms built underground in the archways of the old South Bridge in the 1700s. We learn that these vaults were intended as storage rooms, meant to hold whiskey in oak barrels, wool from Scottish sheep, black tobacco, burlap sacks of grain, and bolts of knotty cloth. But because they were built in a rush, the surface was never sealed and the porous limestone walls seeped Edinburgh's mournful rains right into the stored goods.

So the goods moved out and the poor moved in.

Our guide tells us of the conditions of vaults back then, no better than the rib cage of a swollen carcass. Completely underground, the vaults offer no light to split the pitch black, no fresh air to fill lungs. So undesirable for life that the police stopped monitoring, making it a den for criminals. The bathroom was the corner, the slick-wet floor a bed, and Hope wrapped herself in her cloak and walked out long ago.

In this moment as I look around the vaults, scrubbed clean for the tourist's tender heart, all I can think of is my own bright-eyed daughter, intellectual disabilities woven through her DNA, and how these are the places the disabled ended up in. Now my breaths come fast. I am wondering about all the lives lived in this shattered abyss and find myself uttering a panicked prayer for the dead because I don't know what else to do with all this sadness filling my lungs, my heart, my throat.

I know now is not then, but also, is it? I wonder, given the chance, would we have stopped it? Three hundred years later, have we evolved, changed, grown?

At the grocery store a child shouts, "What is that?" while pointing at a wheelchair. The mother says, "Shhh," and rushes away. On the street, a husband puts a protective arm around his wife as a young man passes by, his chin jerking as he grunts. A woman with Down syndrome sits alone at the church potluck, picking at invisible lint on her dress.

We tell ourselves the vaults are ancient history, a relic of an ignorant age, but are we that much better? Can the heart not hold stone cages too?

From that moment many of his disciples turned back and no longer accompanied him. So Jesus said to the Twelve, "You don't want to go away too, do you?" Simon Peter answered, "Lord, to whom will we go? You have the words of eternal life. We have come to believe and know that you are the Holy One of God." JOHN 6:66-69

"Where Else Would I Go?"

I look around at all the people and cannot stop thinking about the insanity of it all. My faith is a vapor. I grope for it but I cannot find it. The doubt is worse than it has ever been. Today I am a lost thing. I wonder if I will fracture on the spot.

//

Do you think I should not admit this? Do you think I am not qualified? Do you now think I am a hypocrite? But is it not more hypocritical to not tell you? We can wonder this together.

//

Is it the problem of evil? Do you wonder if you are truly a Christian? Are you not sure if He is good? Not convinced He exists? Is it a spiritual attack? Are you wrestling with the intellectual case for Christ? Is it childhood trauma? Is it current suffering? Are you just tired?

//

It is all of it. It is none of it. Although I am definitely tired.

//

Surprise! I do not fracture on the spot. I am still here, flesh and bone and heart and soul. I slept 11.5 hours. I don't think I've done that since college. I write. I go on a run. I play Uno with my children. Things are better today.

//

"From that moment many of his disciples turned back and no longer accompanied him. So Jesus said to the Twelve, 'You don't want to go away too, do you?' Simon Peter answered, 'Lord, to whom will we go?'"

//

I am staring at the meadow behind my house. The grasses are bent, hugging one another as they are pulled to the eastern horizon. The sky is a deep blue and I hear thunder rumble in the distance. A deer raises her head. Her ears prick and she listens to the wind. I imagine what it might be like to climb on her tawny back, bend my head low on her neck, and run.

//

Is hoping it is true enough? Is wanting it as reality sufficient? I look around at the other options. Nothing appeals in the slightest. Hope holds my doubts like a cradle. I do not want to go away. I remind myself that I do not have to sort it all out today.

The L*ORD* *is near the brokenhearted;*
he saves those crushed in spirit. PSALM 34:18

The Howl of Heaven

You are asking how to grieve with grace,
how to let your soul break with eternity in
mind. First, fight the pull to say all the right
things, to Mary Poppins the problem with
a spoonful of sugar. Instead, name the pain
what it is. Call it Madness. Call it Fury. Call
it a Shadow-Self. Call it The Grave. Call
it I-don't-know-how-to-live-without-it
Rage. You do not have to parallel park The
Right Answers next to the cliff's edge. You
do not have to hold an umbrella of platitudes
over your sorrow. These days are for being
unmoored, swallowed by salt as you sail the
tar seas. Second, understand that God is not
breakable, as you seem to believe. He knows
the lullaby of grief, He is not afraid of its beat.
He knows we're all just chewing on the pit of
this world hoping to suck out some fruit. So
go ahead, scream the ache until the sun pales
gray. Do it until you are spent. Until you are
empty. Until your sweaty palms have siphoned
every ounce of trembling pain your soft soul
holds into the dirt of this broken Earth.
Today is not all there is, but you can
remember that tomorrow.

A friend loves at all times. PROVERBS 17:17

Instructions on Friendship

Promise me you'll tell me when you need a can of navy beans or black slacks in youth small for a wedding. Promise me you'll text me to watch your goldendoodle and water your petunias while you're on vacation. Promise me you'll tell me about the ways you believe you fail as a mother while we sit on the deck and I will tell you if you are right. (You are wrong.) Promise me you'll text me when you get a promotion at work. We'll order margaritas—no, champagne—at that restaurant where we like to celebrate. Promise me you'll let me stay when you don't know why God does what He does, and I promise I will not be afraid. Promise me you'll call me when you're too overwhelmed to cook and we'll just add rice to make my dinner go further. Promise me you'll tell me when you have a lump and the doctor orders a scan, and I will put one hand on your knee and one hand on the throne of God and beg, and beg, and beg.

A time to weep and a time to laugh; a time to mourn and a time to dance. ECCLESIASTES 3:4

When Grief Is Your Friend

She lies beside you in the bedroom, her hot hands caressing your cheek. She tells you to take all the time you need, and that the world will take care of itself right now. She never says, "Hush," or "Quiet now." She only pats your back and hands you another tissue, unfazed by the splash of your tears on your lap. Grief is a fierce and rough and untamed thing, never leaving you, only moving in and out of the shadows of the room. She hums a hymn as she brings you breakfast in bed, binges shows with you in the afternoon, and closes the curtains on the moon at night. She understands her role as a caretaker and that someday she will not be needed in this way. But for now, she is here, ever-present, her dark eyes soft as she lifts your chin. "Honey," she says, "Take my hand, we'll walk this road together."

Lord, set up a guard for my mouth;
keep watch at the door of my lips. PSALM 141:3

Hush

1.
I am lying in bed thinking of all the words I want to put back into my mouth. I want to swallow whole paragraphs, half questions, loud jokes, poor instruction, and unnecessary caveats. I imagine falling through the linen duvet of my dark bedroom so an abyss can swallow me whole.

2.
We all want to be something in this life, and what I truly want is to be more like the God I serve, but so often all I am is my easy, unthinking, not-trying self. It is my stories, my wisdom, my truths—in a flashing moment of egotism, I forget who I represent, who I serve. *Why am I like this?* I whisper to the stars from the steps of the porch. They do not answer.

3.
How is it that I have already stacked up so much wrong in so little time? What I am trying to say is, I am in a persistent struggle to forget myself and remember God.

4.

I have a headache from crying. M. tells me that I should know better. That I have done this before. That while I do not start things, I *perpetuate* them. He is kind but now my head *and* my heart hurt. Of course, he is right. I never see it coming but before I know it, I am like a caged feral cat, speaking things I do not even know if I believe are true.

5.

I am no longer out to be the best person I can possibly be. I am only asking Him to make me a little better than I was yesterday. So why does it still feel like trying to grasp water in my fist? I open the window and let the autumn breeze in. I let it make me shiver.

You yourself have recorded my wanderings.
Put my tears in your bottle.
Are they not in your book? PSALM 56:8

Tears

Science tells us tears change based on the reason we cry them. For example, tears from chopping onions have a different chemical composition than other types of tears. They're thinner and go away from our faces faster. Tears of emotion have a protein-based hormone that contains *leucine enkephalin*, a painkiller our body releases when we're stressed. They also have a higher viscosity, which means they run down our faces more slowly and stick to the skin more strongly, making our grief more visible to other people.

Our tears are literally trying to ease the pain of our sorrow and tell others we need comfort. Scientists say tears are a signal to others that we are vulnerable. When someone else sees them, they set off emotions of empathy and compassion for the person who is crying.

But I wonder, perhaps, if they are even more a signal to ourselves that we are vulnerable. That we are thin skin and frail bones, and our soft heart still beats. We can try to hide them, stop them, cover them, but in deep grief, they come and come, clinging with all their hot viscosity to our cheeks.

Let them come. They are a marker that you have lived and loved and you have been changed. Someday God Himself will wipe away every tear from your eyes. But until then, the tears tether you. A reminder of the already but not yet, your humanity and your eternity.

LORD, my every desire is in front of you; my sighing is not hidden from you. My heart races, my strength leaves me, and even the light of my eyes has faded. PSALM 38:9-10

There Are Days That You Hate Yourself

You do not like that I said hate.
You are thinking it is not a godly word to use.
We are to "hate sin," to be "hated by the world,"
but we are not to "hate ourselves."

//

Hate: "To feel intense or passionate dislike for someone."
(This, from Webster's.)
And so, even though our Bible says no,
I am right. There are days you hate yourself.
I know this because I have these days too.

//

I am told by a friend that she does not like a book
because she cannot find the redemption.
I tell her this is exactly why I like it.
Because finally, an echo of our own tired lives.

//

You want me to wrap this up, to give you
your redemption.
You want to read in this precious poem
how I will preach the gospel to myself,
to you, to us all.
But some days, the hate days, all I can give you
is this severed bone.

//

Reed bruised. Nerve exposed.
Black alley cat with a paper bag soul.

//

And yet. I know He will find me still.

The one who conceals his sins will not prosper, but whoever confesses and renounces them will find mercy. PROVERBS 28:13

My pastor says an idol is anything you love more than God

and so I begin to count my loves
carefully, each one rolling
in my throat before it is offered
up to Heaven, quivering and unarmed.
Like pheasant flushed
from the underbrush, they shoot
out of my chest and soon
there are too many to track.
My anarchy flies
to join the multitude—just another earthly
vagabond spilling out her brine.

But I have learned there is healing
in this strange ritual. To sort the colossal
caverns of the heart, stack
up the totems, and burn
all of them to the ground.
It is only then you can sweep
out the ash and pray for rain.

Let us consider one another in order to provoke love and good works, not neglecting to gather together, as some are in the habit of doing, but encouraging each other, and all the more as you see the day approaching. HEBREWS 10:24-25

Maybe We Can Meet

I lean against the counter, listening to the couple. It's cool outside, but inside this house the walls are starting to sweat. We are talking about the church. Again. We are talking about our local church but sometimes it switches to greater problems in the American church and I know sometimes we are confusing the two but I say nothing because I want to listen to their story. They are talking through tears.

//

There is a large elm in my yard. Our first summer here we put a swing on one of its few strong branches and M. dug a fire pit next to it. We sat 10 Adirondack chairs in a lazy circle around the pit. "Too many," he said. "Not enough," I said.

//

Recently the world found out a pastor was not who we thought he was. He was everything we couldn't believe. Online, in person, it was all everyone wanted to talk to me about. *Can I still read his books? Can I still recommend them? Can I admit that he was ever helpful in my life at all?* We are all asking the same questions. We are all coming to different answers.

//

Jesus called a fisherman, an extremist Zealot, and a despised publican working for the enemy. Do you not wonder how they got along? I will tell you the secret: They had an allegiance stronger and truer than their political views.

//

M. looks at me with kind eyes and his hand touches mine. "Remember that time, when we were confused and frustrated by the church's decision, but then we talked to the pastor and everything made sense and we felt kinda bad for being upset? This is probably like that time."

It hurts a little, but there is truth there. At some churches—no, not all—but at some it actually does get healthier as you move further in.

//

Maybe we can meet out by the elm where the cicadas sing and the ferns curl up at night. Maybe we can learn to be less angry and more forgiving. Maybe we can remember that the American church isn't exactly the same as our local church and our local church isn't exactly the same as the American church and neither of them have the capability to be perfect and meet all our needs anyway. Maybe we can meet. Maybe we can heal. Maybe the stars will weep with us.

Just as sin came into the world through one man,
and death through sin, and so death spread
to all men because all sinned. ROMANS 5:12, ESV

Someday We Will Be the Ancients

Soon, we will only be a memory. They will read about us, and talk of our small view of the world. They will speak of our history and how little we knew, how we fought and spoiled and chewed on greed. They will wonder if we cared at all about each other, if our hearts were sulfur or lead or another element we have yet to discover. Like us, they will talk of how evolved they are, how they have nurtured progress like a seed, like a newborn colt. It's true they will know more than us, but humanity will still be the same. Black veins pulsing in the half-light, just waiting for a miracle.

They said, "Come, let's build ourselves a city and a tower with its top in the sky. Let's make a name for ourselves; otherwise, we will be scattered throughout the earth." GENESIS 11:4

Humans

fall for Ponzi schemes, have faith
they might win the lottery, wish
on falling stars, and think
that hitting the button
on the elevator multiple times
will make it go faster.

And yet: We believe we are the gods.

Now may the God of peace himself sanctify you completely, and may your whole spirit and soul and body be kept blameless at the coming of our Lord Jesus Christ.

1 THESSALONIANS 5:23, ESV

Making Ready

One day, you will go downstairs and scrub the floor for the last time. You will match the last sock, change the last bulb, and vacuum the last rug. It will be a Tuesday, or an afternoon in October, or a late evening by the fire in winter. You will dust the lamp, with its thrifted accordion shade, and never dust it again. You won't know when each last is coming and you may not even realize it when it does. But there will be an end to this work of the home. Maybe someone will take over the work for you. A brown-eyed daughter, perhaps. Or a red-headed grandson. Maybe you will watch them work from a tattered wingback, your bones aching and vision blurry, or maybe they will have to scramble to complete it because you are gone and off to the next realm.

However it happens, the lasts will come,
the bland beat of this world will cease,
and the finish line will greet your bone-
worn toes. But that time is not right now.
So unravel if you need to, then tend and
water and nurture, and choose to live
most alive right here, right now, as there is
still much work to do.

He made the moon to mark the festivals;
the sun knows when to set. PSALM 104:19

Sometimes I wonder how the sun can rise

in this world with such grief in it. Does
it ever tire of brightening the horizon
only to be met with another war? Was
the eclipse a welcome respite from looking
down on an abandoned child?
Does it wish for clouds when oil
spills into the sea, immigrants are caged,
or twilight's riots still smolder?
Tell me, do you think the sun ever sighs
as God calls its light to break the sky?
Its rays murmuring,
Another day of this. Another day of them.
Or maybe, despite it all, it chooses to rise
each day because it believes, as I do,
that there is still good in this world, there is
still kindness. Maybe it rises again and again,
homesick for us each night,
hoping its light stirs our hearts a little
for who we could be, for the work we have left to do.
Maybe it's a gold promise in the sky,
shining down on all our faces.

ACT II

LISTEN FOR THE HYMNS OF PROMISE

Two men looked out from prison bars,
One saw the mud, the other saw stars.

DALE CARNEGIE

IN THE WINTER, I set a disco ball by the window in our living room so it can catapult rays of sunlight onto the couch, the ceiling, and the horse-head bookends lining the fireplace shelves. It was a $12 online purchase made on a whim, and it brightens my mood by at least a few thousand dollars every winter. As I tell my husband, it's the one thing that keeps me from booking a desperate trip to Hawaii in the middle of a freezing January in Iowa.

My kids often roll it into other parts of the house, so many mornings, I have to go dig it out from under a bed or basement corner, resticking several mirrored squares back on because it was . . . $12. After the reconstructive surgery, I place the disco ball in the sun for it to do its work on my walls, my mood, and my heart.

Joy doesn't always just magically happen—sometimes, we have to hunt for it, like I do with my disco ball. Once we have done the hard work of admitting our pain and grief, it's time to remind ourselves that not everything in the world has gone haywire. There is still good. There is still beauty. There are still common graces. This is why you'll laugh at a joke right after a life-altering medical diagnosis, spot a rainbow after a tornado, or smile at a friend at a funeral. It's why daisies bloom outside the window as a woman miscarries in the shower, birds sing at graveyards, and your friend still brings you a meal, even when you've been unkind.

It's true that in this life we will never be sequestered from suffering or hidden from hardship. But our days are crowded with good things from God, if we only have eyes to see. And on the days we cannot even muster up a smile, we can remember that everything is being used for God's glory and our good. Nothing is wasted with Jesus. This is His promise to us. Even as life shudders all around, He works miracles on our hearts as day by day He makes us a little more like Him.

This is the greatest gift of all—that we would be prepared and ready when He calls us to His eternal city. This world is not our final home, but it simmers with heavenly light. So lift your eyes to the goodness around you and see how grace flies from God's fingertips with every step you take. Wake up to the rays of His good gifts. Be greedy for them. Let them carry you on your journey home.

The LORD *is good to all, and his mercy is over all that he has made.* PSALM 145:9, ESV

On the bad days

it's nice to remember that when someone loses their wedding ring in a park, sometimes a stranger finds it and returns it. It's nice to remember how people build Little Free Libraries on the boulevard, hoping a passerby might fall in love with a book. All is not lost in this world when you remember how from time to time people let you go before them in line or how someone you've never met compliments your scarf or how the UPS driver offers a barking dog a treat and speaks to it gently. The shadows rise when you remember the young boy who held the door open for you and how strangers are willing to donate their liver to someone in need. When unhappiness is underfoot, think of pen pals, animal adoptions, community gardens, accessible spaces for people with disabilities, and how without question, friends will rally to watch each other's children when one is overwhelmed. They are common graces, these acts of kindness. Hymns of promise that crowd the street corners and circle your feet.

The city does not need the sun or the moon to shine on it, because the glory of God illuminates it, and its lamp is the Lamb. REVELATION 21:23

Jars of Sunlight

I am thinking about how we all want to feel spectacular. We want to feel the sun shine on our story for a day, even an hour. Tightly wound by the next decision / phone call / text message / email / conversation over coffee. Will we be a winner? Or the lonely soul sitting alone at home, nursing a grim unwinding of our wrongness?

//

It is high school and the hope is a nice four years reading under the oak trees on campus. It is college and the hope is a fine little cubicle to call ours, with gossip around the water cooler. It is dinner with a kind young man and the hope is a diamond, marriage, and two kids, maybe five. It is motherhood and the hope is a full night of sleep and clean noses in time for church. It is morning and the hope is a hot cup of coffee and, if we're lucky, a muffin.

//

What is it to be given the sun when it sets every day? Its light does not last. You cannot grip it, you cannot put it in a jar on your shelf to gaze at, you cannot swallow it whole to live in your belly, rubbing it when you need a few fingers' worth of joy.

//

Look, I think we may be going about this all wrong, seeking sunlight like a talisman. He has told us the goal, the purpose, the end game. To know Him, to become like Him, and to make His name known to all. The goal isn't college, marriage, children, or survival. The sunlight is a phantom, a shimmering taunt. What we must see is that each hope, satisfied or shattered, is a tool in the Maker's palm, smoothing the edges of these wild things we call lives into the shape of Him. There is nothing to do but lean into His work, living as honestly as we can, knowing it will all be worth far more than a jar of sunlight. For where we're headed there will be no need for sun, His light will be all we see.

He has made everything appropriate in its time. ECCLESIASTES 3:11

“Good Things Take Time”

You roll your eyes at this phrase, wearing your impatience on your sleeve. But have you forgotten how every year softens and frees your favorite pair of jeans? Or how the oak in the backyard gets more wobbled and gnarled each year? Maybe you never realized how long it takes for a mountain to rise / a diamond to form / a child to grow. I'm guessing you haven't seen my leather tote, supple with memory after seven years on my arm. Or how about cast-iron skillets / the Grand Canyon / your brother's favorite whiskey? Perhaps the Leaning Tower of Pisa slipped your mind, but it is getting a little straighter every year. Or have you ever seen a terra-cotta pot? The patina a requirement for any self-respecting Italian villa.

You feel these examples do not help, because you are thinking about your life and all that you hoped for. But look at how long it took for me to experience serendipity for the first time. To learn to package and swallow my pride. To write this poem. Lightbulb moments are always few and far between. I'm still working on cracking the code to wisdom / self-acceptance / emotional consistency / early bedtimes.

You want the world now, no matter the rage and grief and love, but don't rush your small feet on this big Earth. Here, savor the crush of the blackberry between your teeth. Look at your plum-faced child out the window. Feel your hair tangle as the wind gallops toward the sunset. It's time that shapes us into who we should be. All we can do is linger in its ebbs and flows, expectant and a bit breathless for what it will bring.

We know that all things work together for the good of those who love God, who are called according to his purpose. For those he foreknew he also predestined to be conformed to the image of his Son, so that he would be the firstborn among many brothers and sisters. ROMANS 8:28-29

The Bad Thing

Maybe it is not
that we have received
a Bad Thing, but that
the Bad Thing
has produced
all these Very Good Things.

The sickness producing compassion.
The job loss, courage.
The disability, humility.
The broken friendship, clarity.
The failed dream, resilience.
The death, a hope of Heaven.

You do not have to be grateful
for the Bad Thing, but can
you see the ways it has been
redeemed and resurrected
into the Very Good Things?
All those lost pieces
of your life reshape and grow
you, a mysterious exchange
of grief for glory.

Only goodness and faithful love will pursue me all the days of my life, and I will dwell in the house of the LORD as long as I live. PSALM 23:6

What if

we have it all wrong
and hope still lives
even in the midst of our unbearable grief?
Hang on, let's just look at your life,
glowing like the northern lights.
They say that some days,
the aurora can't be seen by the human eye,
but a camera lens can still pick it up.

Maybe this is like His still waters,
all around you—you're cradled
in the soft waves—
yet your eyes can't see it.
But I can.
You're sailing His silver seas
straight to the harbor,
goodness and mercy stream behind you.
The water shimmers in gold.

The other disciples were telling him, "We've seen the Lord!" But he said to them, "If I don't see the mark of the nails in his hands, put my finger into the mark of the nails, and put my hand into his side, I will never believe." JOHN 20:25

The Offering

Thomas missed the first twilight showing of scars,
delayed, maybe, by a herd of sheep on the road.
So instead, Jesus came to Thomas in the deep heat
of the afternoon and said, "Put your finger here."
The raised, round knot pulsed in his palm.
And Thomas obeyed, his eyes searching
Jesus' face for recognition.

Next, Jesus untied His belt, let it fall to the floor.
He reached His scarred hands to the hem
of His tunic, lifting higher and higher
until a red, angry scar on His belly
appeared, the exact size of a Roman spear.
"Reach out your hand and put it into my side,"
Jesus said. Thomas's fingers shook
as he felt the new spiderweb skin,
taut with scarlet stain.
He gently brushed it with his thumb,
each rough ridge causing his ribs to pinch.

"My Lord and my God!" Thomas gasped,
surprise covering his face like a constellation.
Jesus' head tilted back and He roared with laughter.
He pulled Thomas in for a hug, gave him two slaps
on the back like a victor.
Then He straightened and His voice dropped,
and He told the room those who are
unlike Thomas will be blessed.
Thomas wasn't bothered, there was no shame
in Jesus' tone. Thomas had what he needed now,
so he tucked it deep in the pocket
of the tunic his mother made for him.

Sometime, in the distant future, Thomas
would replay the memory as he watched
the frogs in the riverbank,
their legs coiling and pushing off the wet rocks.
Word of his doubt was spreading
but he didn't mind.
"Whatever it takes," he murmured. And he tossed
a rock in the water as he walked away.
Could he have known that thousands of years
later, we'd all still be learning from him?

I was sleeping, but my heart was awake. A sound! My love was knocking. SONG OF SONGS 5:2

I wonder when it was that I fell more in love with you?

Was it when you rose out of bed to check
the house because I heard a noise?
Was it that time you swapped out the glass
pendants over the island for me? Was it when
we took a last-minute trip
to Paris and we ate croissants
on the train to Versailles?
I wonder if it was all the times
you have sat on the kitchen counter
like a king, shelling pistachios and talking to me,
while the kids ran with the dog in the living room.

I am thinking it could be the time you picked
up my parents from the airport late at night,
or when you sat and plucked out Coldplay
on the piano, your ear cocked to the side
as you listened for the right notes. It could
be the time you moved
all the couches and vacuumed
under the rugs. You wore headphones
and you sang the entire time. Maybe
it was tonight as you held
our restless daughter in the dark nursery.
I asked you the time when you came back.
"3 a.m.," you whispered as you lifted
the comforter. You came into my warmth
and I knew, I just fell a little more in love with you.

I am certain that I will see the LORD's goodness in the land of the living. PSALM 27:13

What Motherhood Taught Me

One day, you may be crying
in the bathroom or lying
sick on the couch. Or maybe
you are feeling like this world
is just too much and you have
had more than enough,

when suddenly the front door bursts
open bringing with it your child's
moon face, freckles like brown sugar
on her flushed cheeks. Her small fist,
full of wild daises, pushes
toward your nose.

For you, she says, oblivious
to your stale state. You see,
in motherhood, good happens,
even when you don't plan for it, even
when you think it is not
possible. It blooms curiously
between the wood slats
of your living room floor, peeks
out from beneath the bedsheets, and blows
through your front door. There is
no end to its invitation. It is simply
up to you to receive it.

The Lord *your God is among you, a warrior who saves. He will rejoice over you with gladness. He will be quiet in his love. He will delight in you with singing.* ZEPHANIAH 3:17

November

It was morning and the children
were lined up
at the counter in the kitchen.
Bagels warmed
in the toaster and November's
tender skies bloomed blue
out the window. School
was on break
so we took one too.

You were perched
on the counter, humming
that new song we love.
Somewhere
in the middle of the debate
between cream cheese
and peanut butter, I stepped out

of myself. It was
at that moment,
I knew. Everything
was as it should be.
The heaviness of it all
suspended,
    bearable.

And for one precious
pulse, I saw it.

This life is everything
we hoped for.
You came up
behind me
at the sink. You put
your hands on my hips.

The sweetness of a friend is better than self-counsel. PROVERBS 27:9

Pioneers

We trade bags of carrots for cans of beans,
a loaf of homemade bread for a frozen pizza.
We are pioneers trading goods over text.
We talk of when to trim the hydrangeas,
who has extra soccer cleats, and what
fourth-grade teacher to ask for. We are
YouTube and Yelp and Facebook Marketplace.

We pass our children back and forth and
declare ourselves *auntie.* Group snacks
are at 3:30 p.m. We are daycare and teachers,
mentors and second mothers.

We remind each other we are allowed
to lie on the couch when we are sick,
to be sad that our husbands work late,
to serve snack plates at dinner.
We talk of the childhood we wish we had.
Of the marriages we keep. Of the children we hope for.

We hold each other's shoulders in the driveway,
blouses at the hospital, children at the funeral.
This must be what it means, I think,
when the church says we should *do life together*.
To stand beside the ones who say, "I see you and I am not afraid."

For it was you who created my inward parts; you knit me together in my mother's womb. PSALM 139:13

DNA

You'll catch your death there, standing
by that window. Here, take my cardigan.
Take this tea. I made it with honey. Your hooded
eyes tell me that you cannot stand yourself again.

Did you know I read if you took all your DNA
and straightened it out, it would stretch to Jupiter
and back? And not just once, but 10 times.
All those genes tucked inside your skin would stretch nearly a billion miles

if you let them out.

And so here I am, looking at you and thinking
of all that I love. One, your tenderness toward children.
Two, how you love to listen to the rain. Three,
how you play the piano softly. Sometimes
I like to think of God making us. Knitting, linking,
lacing, compressing all those rows of DNA into
marrow and muscle, finger and face.

There are many pulls to be unhappy this side of Eden,
but who He made you is not one of them. Honestly,
I am not surprised that the stuff that makes you
who you are would fill the universe.

We have spoken openly to you . . . ; our heart has been opened wide. 2 CORINTHIANS 6:11

Voyager

You woke up wondering if you were
a little too honest last night.
If you gave up too much of yourself.
You are worried about what they will think.
    What they will remember.
                    What they will get wrong.
        What they will get *right.*
The term you are looking for
is "vulnerability hangover." Though
you are trying, a hot cup of coffee will not fix it.

Yet what you have done is a lost art.
We were towers of stones, cracking
and splitting, as you opened up
your heart and said, "Take everything."
You voyaged first into the delicious, unknown
land and we followed. I am trying
to tell you thank you for making us less alone.

Therefore encourage one another and build each other up as you are already doing. 1 THESSALONIANS 5:11

The Language of Friendship

Holding her drink / jacket / boundaries / griefs / child. Afternoon walks around the lake / neighborhood sidewalk / city streets / her heart. Wearing the same shoes / pants / makeup / purse / convictions and always being a bit surprised. Picking up her puppy / Costco order / children / shattered hopes. Carrying her sweater / credit card / dreams / memories. Borrowing a cup of flour / dress for a date / steamer / serving dishes for a party / her hope-filled heart. Helping her purge her closets / gardens / ghosts / shame. Recommending doctors / recipes / cocktails / beach reads / peace. Asking about her skin care routine / weekend plans / husband / scars. Traveling together for vacations / concerts / errands / school parties / life.

She never says it exactly, but all of it says, *I love you, I am here, and you are not alone.*

When all has been heard, the conclusion of the matter is this: fear God and keep his commands, because this is for all humanity. ECCLESIASTES 12:13

Live and Let Live

Have you noticed how the peony bush never tries to tame its creamsicle blossoms? Or how the elm reaches its ribboned branches as wide as it can? My golden dog fans out over half the length of the couch, belly up, just in case a passerby might be inclined to rub it. "Nature just wants to live," my friend says as she helps me plant the summer garden. *She is right*, I think. It does not worry if its bloom is untamed or if its branches take up too much space or if it's told, *That is enough—no more, be smaller.* The hind does not worry about the shape of its leg or if its warm doe eyes look tired. Nature only wants you to notice it, to savor the pleasure of its full figure and heartbreaking form. It begs you to watch the gray goose fly south to warmth, to be surprised by the prairie chicken rupturing from the grasses, to track the chestnut mare as she runs and bucks. Each day my dog exposes his heart, beating in his ribs, as his amber eyes meet mine: *Be kind to yourself, live well.*

For the eyes of the LORD roam throughout the earth to show himself strong for those who are wholeheartedly devoted to him. 2 CHRONICLES 16:9

Secret Lives

There is a candle burning on the kitchen counter, a woman looks over her to-do list. Scarlet lines deepen on the tomatoes at the neighbors' while an abandoned stick of blue chalk rolls down the sidewalk after a sudden gale. A man rubs his sore knee before he pushes off the floral bed quilt and shuffles to the bathroom. Downstairs his elderly wife stirs soup on the stove, licking the spoon to check for salt. Outside a teen narrowly misses a squirrel as he speeds down the curving road. The squirrel's heart beats double time as it returns to its mossy nest to nuzzle its kits. Rainwater sits in a pool nearby, a grasshopper bristles, splintering the reflection. In a car, a woman cries after hanging up the phone, her freckles glistening like summer stars. Nearby, a child sticks a finger through the hole of her pink polka-dot sock, then throws it in the grass. She walks to the edge of the backyard hill and stands with her arms bent, like a tiny superhero surveying her kingdom. So many secrets no one sees, no one hears.

Except Him. His eyes rove to and fro
over all the earth, never missing a thing.

ACT III

UNBUTTON YOUR HEART

I am a little weary of my life—Not thy life, blessed Father!

GEORGE MACDONALD, *DIARY OF AN OLD SOUL*

I WAS FLOATING on a boat somewhere in the middle of the Pacific Ocean when I saw my first blue whale. I shaded my eyes from the sun while I watched it announce its arrival with a 30-foot plume of water. Reaching lengths of up to 100 feet, the blue whale is the largest animal on the planet. Its tongue alone weighs as much as a small elephant. Its main artery, the aorta, is so big and round, you could toss a cello in it. And perhaps most impressive of all, the blue whale's heart weighs nearly 1,300 pounds and is about the size of a 10-person hot tub. Each year, the blue whale migrates thousands of miles through the ocean while essentially carrying around the weight of a grand piano in its chest.

And I wonder if that's how many of us spend our days: our frail human frames bearing burdened hearts that feel as heavy as a small car. Life's pain, suffering, and regrets stack up like storage containers until we wonder if we might be crushed. Hands clasped to our chest to keep it all in, we're just barely keeping it all together. So what are we to do?

It is something that is very easy but at the same time very hard. Once we have acknowledged the ache and spotted glimmers of hope, we must loosen our grip on our chest and let it all spill out at the base of the cross. We must let Christ have everything. It is very easy because all we need to do is say *yes* with humility. But it is also very hard because it means we must let go of control and let Him take over. We must trust God with our entire life.

But the good news is, He is worthy of our trust. This is why Christ went to the cross, to pay for our sin and wrongdoings so we could know Him as a Father and friend. If we say *yes*, Jesus will prove His love for us over and over again. But know, too, that we must also consistently confess and surrender our failures and offenses, for they will continue as long as we labor on this Earth. Following Jesus is not one-and-done, but a regular rhythm of coming before Him, unbuttoning our heart, and letting Him bring everything back to order.

There will be times our heart will still feel heavier than a literal blue whale's, but when we are in Christ, He will carry the weight for us. So let's allow our hands to fall to our sides in surrender. Let's trust Him with our whole heart and say, "Not my will, but yours be done." That's all we need to do right now. He'll take care of the rest.

Encourage each other daily, while it is still called today. HEBREWS 3:13

These Days

1.
These days I am waiting for the peonies to appear and the boxwoods to grow. I am driving the children to school and taking them to piano. I am plugging in the Crock-Pot and unplugging the laptop. I am going to church and drinking tea at book club. I am okay.

2.
"We are all in a mental health crisis. Every single person in America is in a mental health crisis right now!" The podcaster rants for at least five minutes straight before the music begins, and I realize I am holding my breath. This is the kind of thing, I think, that creates a mental health crisis in America.

3.
We are all told that "we are not okay." It is poured down our open mouths and thrust into our waiting chests. "Political unrest, a war, a teetering economy—how could anyone be fine? And of course, there are children. Who can possibly parent and not lose their minds?"

4.

I look around the room. Here is a fireplace, here is a stack of books, here is my husband, here are my three children. It is achingly beautiful. Have you ever felt this, like everything is right in the world because for one second—even just one—it is right in your own home? Yes, you know there is pain and injustice and suffering but there is also love and friendship and books?

5.

I have been told to be gentle with myself. I am trying.

6.

L. says the most helpful and healing thing a therapist can do is to be an empathetic, compassionate witness to someone's story. I believe him because he is my friend. You can believe him because he has a PhD and a book on emotions, theology, and psychology. It won an award.

7.

We are all trying to be better at living. We are all asking God to make it easier, make it better, make it all work out. Medicine and therapy and counselors and hotlines and online comfort creators—"God, just use one of them, any of them." Maybe He will. But maybe what He will use is each other. Maybe what we need is, *How are you? / How did it go? / And then what happened? / Tell me more. / I'm sorry. / I love you.*

God has not given us a spirit of fear, but one of power, love, and sound judgment. 2 TIMOTHY 1:7

Control Freak

I am sitting in my second session
of counseling and the therapist asks
me to identify my core negative belief.
I quickly scan the list and "I am not
in control" pops off the page like a billboard.
She tells me the belief we're going to replace
it with is "I am now in control." I chuff
a laugh and tell her I know the realities
of this life, the curse of the fall, the brokenness
of the world. Control is a vapor.
My daughter has disabilities, my dad
has Parkinson's, and I have chronic pain that no doctor
can fix. And that's just the first three
that ripple to the top. She smiles at me
and says, "We'll talk about it."

Turns out we never really talk about it,
but as we work through the landscape
of my life, I begin to see what she means.
While it is true that life is a briar patch,
she shows me that I can still choose
how I respond to its thorns. But it is hard
to make good, Spirit-led choices
when you always feel like you are on the brink
of war with the world. It is hard to believe
you have power over anything—
let alone your responses—when injustice's
train has made too many stops in your life
and you are the exception to the statistics.
And yet I know it's worth a try.
To heal and believe and trust the God I love
to guide me and bring me peace.
In many ways, control is still a myth.
But that little sliver that's mine?
Give it to me like a slice of an overripe Missouri
peach in summer. Let me suck it dry.

I will come to the altar of God,
to God, my greatest joy. PSALM 43:4

Joy

Some days I don't know how to be anything
but sad. All I can think about
is all I don't have and all I do have
and how nothing landed in the right spot.
The truth is, I have walked across the world
and it is mostly loss and grief and tenderness
and politics. But then I think of Joy and His
infinite love and how He keeps making sure
I bump into joy even when my eyes are down
and my knees are tucked. I do not know much
but I do know that we all want joy to be singalongs
and streamers and celebrations, and sometimes
it is. But mostly joy is sitting on the porch
and goodnight kisses and English ivy winding
around the deck railings. It is family dinners, french fries,
art projects, and trampolines. It is stealing a glance,
holding a hug, and not being afraid of hard questions.
It is forgiveness and compassion and holding your thumb
to your throat and feeling the thump, thump, thump,
knowing you did nothing to make it happen.
It's waking up each morning and recognizing
it's a miracle to believe in Joy at all.

By the grace of God I am what I am, and his grace toward me was not in vain. 1 CORINTHIANS 15:10

Hold This

It is possible to hold two truths
in your hands; each one a tyrant.
It is possible to be tired and happy.
To feel anger and love.
To be lonely yet surrounded.
It is like how a baby can be crying
and nothing is wrong. How the soft, curved
female form is made of iron, flame.
How the raging child is only asking
you to stay, to sit, to sing.
I wonder, then, why do your shoulders droop
and your eyes dim when you are imperfect?
You are still a good mother.
Here, let me put that in your hand.

When David had finished speaking with Saul,
Jonathan was bound to David in close friendship,
and loved him as much as he loved himself. 1 SAMUEL 18:1

Don't Mind Me

What I want is the kind of friendship
that doesn't mind a stack of socks
and a coffee ring on the table.
A friendship that holds up the muffin tin
with crumbs still crusted on and laughs
about how *it happens to me too.*
I want a friendship that walks the yard together,
debating whether the wisteria is still well.
A friendship that sits with my sick child while I shower,
and isn't afraid when I confess my doubts about God.
I want a friendship that pulls out the paper plates,
pours their own water, doesn't wear makeup, and texts,
"Do we like this dress?" while in the dressing room.
I want a friendship that says, *Remember when? /*
I've told you this before / You already know this, but.
What I want is the kind of friendship
that doesn't mind me in your world,
because I so desperately want you in mine.

I want very much to see you, so that I may impart to you some spiritual gift to strengthen you, that is, to be mutually encouraged by each other's faith, both yours and mine. ROMANS 1:11-12

What I Am Thinking About

If you ask me what I am thinking about,
I might say the smell of last night's
chocolate cake, or maybe how it rains
diamonds on Neptune. I might mention
how the alyssum is coming along
delightfully in the summer garden, or
how I am thinking about trying
my hand at sourdough.

It is all true, but it is Easy.

Or, if you ask me what I am thinking about,
I may tell you how I have seen that the human
heart can break at any moment,
or how God always replies in kindness,
even when I am not kind to Him. Maybe
I would tell you of the cracked earth
of a friendship I am trying to water,
or how I need two hands to count
today's griefs alone.

It is all true, but it is Hard.

If you ask me what I am thinking about,
I might wonder which you would want: the
Easy or the Hard. I suppose
I only know what I would want from you: both.

I would want all of it.

Iron sharpens iron, and one person sharpens another. PROVERBS 27:17

Last night's dream was a museum of my childhood—

you were there and it's like I've lived twice. When we were girls, I mostly saw you on Sundays, floral dress and stick-straight hair. You'd whisper jokes in my ear when the teacher turned to the flannel board to reposition Paul. When I complained about anything, you'd tell me, "That's just life," even though we were only eight. But when I broke my wrist doing a swan dive off your bunk bed, you brought me a bag of frozen peas and spoke to me with tenderness.

I can't visit you like I once could, just a quick drive north up the road. Now you have a husband and four kids, lawn care and bills, all in another state. But sometimes, when I am alone, I hear the whisper of pages rustling and you telling me to *trust Him*, in a voice like an ache, like love that is too earnest to be soft. Could I have known what you would be to me when we were so young? Could I have known it would be your words in my mind when my cheeks are wet? I suppose this is the way of it all, keeping only once you've let go. Never knowing what will remain. What will be truly yours.

Having the eyes of your hearts enlightened, that you may know what is the hope to which he has called you, what are the riches of his glorious inheritance in the saints. EPHESIANS 1:18, ESV

The Walk

Come, let us trade stories of pain.
I will tell you how I could not have seen it coming.
How I am up at night watching the replay.
You will tell me how you should have known better.
How you study it like a cipher when no one is looking.

Our mistakes are everywhere, a constellation of failure.
We struggle to learn, to grow, to become.
"Did it have to go this way?" we murmur over coffee.
Perhaps. Perhaps not.

Yet maybe it is not *What could we have done?*
But *What do we do now?*
You will tell me we are to trust Him.
And I will tell you the same.

We will send out an army for each other,
finding the sun in the indigo dark.
We will shape a refuge from its rays.
as we walk each other to the cross.

When you were dead in trespasses . . . he erased the certificate of debt, with its obligations, that was against us and opposed to us, and has taken it away by nailing it to the cross. COLOSSIANS 2:13-14

The Replay

There is a moment each night when you take a bit of time to replay your failures and mistakes of the day. After dinner perhaps. Or when you are brushing your teeth. During this time, you don't like who you are, so you're wishing you were Sally across the street or Linda from the PTA, because of course, they are perfect. You give yourself a short lecture on the importance of being sensitive to others' needs and how you should not speak every thought you have. You remind yourself how you wanted to work on being humble and self-controlled. Your hand moves to the familiar throb in your chest, rubbing the pain that reminds you of your stress and worry and utter inability to do anything right. You feel your misery up to your teeth for a few minutes, an hour. Then something makes you forget. TV. A book. Sleep.

I have done this routine many times, and I can tell you it is entirely understandable, natural in fact! Punishing yourself certainly seems to be the right route to go. But might I suggest another way? One that is harder, even counterintuitive, but it does not require betrayal and misery (and I think it can even help with that pain in your chest).

Here is what you do: Each night, patiently receive the replay. Feel the wrongness. Know its truth. Remove its lies. When you have done this, when you have learned what you can, bring it all right over here, to the base of the cross. Set it there carefully, and—this will be hard!—walk away. Yes, that's right. Just turn around and walk away, 180 degrees. Don't worry. This was always the plan. His love took care of it long ago.

Don't you see? You have this one, grand life. In Him, you are allowed to live it lightly.

He said to me, "It is done! I am the Alpha and the Omega, the beginning and the end. To the thirsty I will give from the spring of the water of life." REVELATION 21:6, ESV

The thing is,

what will bring you true
happiness in this world
can seem so small and unseen,
you often pass it right by.
Your eyes are fixed on the trick
of a rainbow's end,
your belly burning with want
for a flickering crown.
But true happiness will not snap
for your attention, it will not turn
your cheeks with a nudge and plead.
Its welcome simply persists in its pure
and tender way. Here, look into this well,
see the spring that flows freely there?
It is up to you to peel your eyes
from the mirage and *drink.*

For I satisfy the thirsty person and feed all those who are weak. JEREMIAH 31:25

Mulberries

Someday soon we'll walk the path in the woods
that we like so much. We'll stop and stuff mulberries
into our mouths until our laughter is stained purple.
We'll dance by the river and you'll hum
your favorite tune in my ear.
For a time we'll forget the groans of the weary world,
the poisoned arrow of pain.
We'll see that the minnows still play
under the light of the water and the bluebells still charm
the steep banks of the creek.
Then we'll look up to see the fat, jubilant sparrow
fly through the oaks. And we'll remember
what has been true all along:

He cares, He cares.

The Spirit of God has made me, and the breath of the Almighty gives me life. JOB 33:4

Each morning, I study my pinky to see if it shakes.

They say it often starts there, Parkinson's. For more than a decade I have watched the disease as it leisurely, gently acquires my father's body. The doctors say it will continue in its unhurried way, devouring his strength, his gait, his autonomy, and perhaps even his mind.

//

Who has not seen a poison in someone they love? Defenseless bodies succumbing to the plucking of the petals of life. Falling, one by one by one, until the body, a husk.

//

Look, are you wondering, like I am, what to do when there is no hope for relief, here under the dying stars?

//

I drive my mom and dad home from the clinic. My mother crosses her legs in the back seat. My father turns to smile at me and pats my leg. *Oh Lord, if it happens to me, may I endure like him.*

//

These diseases don't offer much for a swan song. Only the chance to be brave. To wake up each morning—despite life's bruises—as a beating heart of evidence that life is worth living and God is still good and worth trusting.

The heart of man plans his way, but the LORD establishes his steps. PROVERBS 16:9, ESV

One Day

Today, someone will get married. Another will have a baby. Someone else will get a ring while he is on one knee. Today, someone will get a promotion at work, and another will finally gather their courage to leave and make their own fortune. Someone will buy their first house, someone will be the first in their family to graduate from college, and someone will retire, leaving the crush of the city for afternoons at the beach. Today, someone will meet their health goals after two long years of effort. Someone else will lock in that vacation to Hawaii they've spent the last five years saving for. Someone will finish their DIY home remodel or pay off their hospital bill or self-publish their first book. Today, someone will ring a bell: finally, cancer-free. Someone else will show their mettle to sign up for therapy, another will realize at long last their anxiety hasn't called, and still another will quit their addiction for good.

Take heart, dear friend, one of these days
that someone could be you.

God is enthroned above the circle of the earth; its inhabitants are like grasshoppers. He stretches out the heavens like thin cloth and spreads them out like a tent to live in. ISAIAH 40:22

When Life Isn't Fair

Climb to the top of the hill, up, up, up, and feel
the rush of the wind on your cheeks. Eyes like a bird's,
hunt for goldenrod in the meadow.
Stand under the walnut tree and listen
to the language of rain on its leaves.
Haunt the moon at night and gather
its stars in your fist. Pluck an orange from the bowl,
stick your thumb in, and lick off its sweet juice.
Walk the edge of the sea during low tide
and see how it makes the earth bigger, even just for a time.

The heavens declare the glory of God, and the expanse proclaims the work of his hands. PSALM 19:1

This Side of the Sky

In the morning, I search for God behind the sun. I think He must smile at this, and sometimes sigh. Spiritual alchemy—I search for Him in my telescope of faith, ravenous as a robin at dawn.

//

S. tells me I am too focused on the Heavens. *God will not make you hunt*, she says. I nod in agreement, though if I am honest, some days it is hard to sense the heat of His hand holding mine as He leads me over the shell of this world.

//

Even though I know He is here, I still find myself staring hard at the sky. His Word tells me to look for the day when I will unhook from the rope of this Earth and fly, palms out with offering, to finally see my King as He makes all things new—like the Siberian iris erupting from the spring garden or at the first, delicious note of a song.

//

Though S. tells me *There's no need*, I like imagining God stepping out from behind the great star when I pray and leaning His ear down low to the chest of this Earth to catch my small sorrows in His hands.

//

Truth be told, there are a million places to look for God, and I have discovered you can find Him in every one.

//

I am learning to remind myself, as many times as I need, that I am elbow to elbow with God this side of the sky. He is here with me as I sweep this porch, hold this child, sway with my husband in this kitchen. In the in-between I will receive what He gives, in the way He has chosen, at the time He has decided to give it.

//

That does not mean I do not still ache for the other side.

INTERMISSION

A MOMENT TO ADDRESS THE BODY IN THE ROOM

I had youth and hope. I believe, beauty. It matters very little now.

CHARLES DICKENS, BLEAK HOUSE

IF YOU ARE A WOMAN, you will need no explanation for why we need to acknowledge the body in the room, but I will offer one anyway. Like most females, I have struggled with accepting certain parts of my body for most of my life. Each new cultural message around embracing a positive body image brings with it the hint of salvation from my torturous thoughts, but as time goes on, each movement has fallen apart like a cheap sweater. For we women have found it impossible to hold to the standard of waiflike figures or sculpted sylphs. And who could learn to love their cellulite or be proud of their pimples? What about those of us with chronic pain or a disability or a degenerative disease—how do we reconcile these ideals with bodies that don't do what we ask?

The world has yet to find a satisfactory answer. But the gospel has a perfect one. Being made in God's image, we know that our bodies were made intentionally and thoughtfully by our Creator. But because of the fall, they don't always work or look the way they're supposed to. It's right and good to acknowledge this and realize that we do not have to love every part of our bodies, because not every part of our bodies is lovable—and our bodies do not determine our value. Instead, we can praise God for the things that are right and true about them, while also acknowledging the hardships and struggles.

It is when we arrive at this point that we can finally have freedom from the nagging and dissatisfaction over our bodies. When we give our body image and self-worth to the Lord, we see how—though there are things we would change if we could—He is using everything to make us more like Him and for His glory. The chronic pain has perhaps produced in you a long-suffering spirit; the thin hair, compassion or maybe humility; and the soft stomach, an identity rooted in your Savior, rather than a six-pack.

When we operate out of a place of knowing we are fully valued, loved, and declared beautiful by our Creator, we see our bodies not as a sign of our morality but as a tool to steward for the good of others, as long as God gives us life. So eat the cake. And the veggies. If you're able to, go for a walk. And take a nap. When all else fails, go out and stand under the night sky. Scientists estimate there are up to 400 billion stars in our galaxy alone. Tell God exactly how you feel. Then look up. There are 400 billion tiny *I love you*s shining right above your head.

I will not set before my eyes anything that is worthless. PSALM 101:3, ESV

Bridled

I dream I am Aphrodite,
long legs, long hair, long stares.
Hips like a full moon
and curves like a pineapple,
all lust and pleasure.

When I wake, the goddess
is a memory, and I'm still me.
Plain as paper. Invisible as air.
Feeling like the dirt
from which I came.

I suppose when you
spend your life nibbling
on mud and dust, your ribs
will always ache, your palms
will always spread for more.

Unfortunately for the world,
contentment doesn't sell.
Spit on the bit and chewing
on lies, bridled is best.
Aphrodite, their carrot.

What I know is this:
Since Eden, we women
always want what we don't
have, when all we need
is already ours.

He will transform the body of our humble condition into the likeness of his glorious body, by the power that enables him to subject everything to himself. PHILIPPIANS 3:21

Today I woke up hoping to find another woman in this body.

A woman who is not me, but is flowered and fairy-like, all mustang and magic. Utterly good. This woman makes wise choices, like selecting salads, holding her tongue and temper, and carefully applying anti-wrinkle creams at night. But when the sunlight hit my sheets, I was disappointed. It was still me in this claustrophobic body, wondering how to live a life I can never live. I swear I felt Eve sitting on my chest, a feral grin on her bird-face, whispering, *No one escapes the devil, baby.* But then I was up and the bone-eyes of Eve were gone and I remembered with soft comfort that it is not yet time. That someday—I confess I don't know when—ancient rules will awaken, like sudden lightning or a phoenix screaming into flight, and this reckless, howling hope will no longer be just hope but reality. On that day, I will do only good, there behind the golden gates. Now I am standing at the sink and I tuck my hair behind my ear, sighing into the inky sea of my reflection. I won't deny that I am tired. But I can see it. A bright future.

Brothers and sisters, in view of the mercies of God, I urge you to present your bodies as a living sacrifice, holy and pleasing to God; this is your true worship. ROMANS 12:1

Stunner

All the years you spent
with sweaty legs in 90-degree heat
because you didn't want the world to see
the dimples in your thighs.
And how it turned out
no one cared about the form
of your knees or the lack of a thigh gap,
because they were all too caught up
in their own perceived insufficiencies.
What we never think about is how
you don't need a particular pant size
to coach third-grade soccer. Or a smooth forehead
to embrace a friend's grief on your shoulder.
You don't need a beach body
to rock a child in the dark of the night
or lean arms to offer a gentle smile
to the grocery store clerk.
God does not require you to have a sylphlike figure to watch
the stars arrange themselves in the sky
or for you to gasp a little at the way they shine.

I am sure of this, that he who started a good work in you will carry it on to completion until the day of Christ Jesus. PHILIPPIANS 1:6

The way we suck our soft stomachs in.

The way we cover our corncob thighs and cedar trunk waists at the swimming pool. The way we say, *Beauty is pain* to our daughters as we compress the air in our lungs. The way we don't have an answer for their round eyes when we put on our morning makeup.

//

The way we grip our rib cages and silence our marrow when we walk into a room. The way we wonder if others are thinking about our body too. Are we too large, too round, too soft, too thick? Do we take up too much space? The way we believe there is a limit.

//

Unfold these thoughts and listen to me. Think of the women we admire—it is not the way their straight noses lie or their young hands wrap around their waists. It is the way their leather fingers knead the dough on the butcher-block counter. The way their words, ordinary, meek, give life as we walk along dirt roads. The way their aged, calloused knees crack and fold to pray, their strong, honeyed voices lift to sing.

//

Steady your breath now and hold my hand. Linger by the banks of the river, marveling at the emerald feathers of the mallard. Let the laughter startle you as it bubbles out of your throat. Say a prayer of thanks for this earthen vessel, holding who you will become.

Be imitators of God, as dearly loved children. EPHESIANS 5:1

Reflection

It is morning and I am thinking
about what I might do to cover
the dark circles under my eyes.
I have been told that I "look young,"
but today, even in the dim lights, I know I look old.
I wonder, reader, if you will allow me to admit
that I have granted too much thought
to how I might pocket eternal youth.
In the early twilight I have fantasized—

new nose,
new lips,
new face—

how much time have I wasted
on these wishes, hunting down a phantom god?
A grand master of the game, the snake hovers, curled
like a question mark, waiting to hiss, "Checkmate."
Oh Lord, let me learn to live
in these good bones. I study the face in the mirror,
knowing out of all the gods I cradle,
God is the only one I truly want.
I utter a prayer that each day,
I only look a little more like Him.

Indeed, we groan in this tent, desiring to put on our heavenly dwelling. 2 CORINTHIANS 5:2

These Bitter Bones

When I was eight, my dog spied a rabbit on our walk and yanked the leash so hard and fast he dislocated my collarbone. Before we left on the walk, my dad told me, *Whatever you do, don't let go of the leash.* I was always an obedient child. That was the first time my body knew the scream of true pain. These days, when it's particularly cold outside, I can still hear its echo.

In my first meeting with my therapist, she asks me to name everywhere I feel physical pain and describe what it feels like. I list them out, eventually becoming uncomfortable with the length of invisible fires smoldering beneath my skin. I even forget about two. And I didn't even mention the ones, like my collarbone, with cries that come and go.

I am told by many doctors and specialists that I worked my body too hard in my early 30s. I simply asked her for too much. I admit, I remember her bleating protest and I just fed her caffeine and mental fortitude while telling her to *hush*. Now I am trying to pay penance, but she is bitter.

I know it is such a short time that we have together on this Earth, my body and I. I want to make peace with her, to drop this anchor we carry, but we are both a bit wary. Yet we are only guaranteed each other and a distant hope of a coming cosmic miracle for us both—body and soul.

Sometimes I forget His salvation is for her too.

I close my bedside drawer filled with pain pills. It is still dark this morning, the night lingering a little more each day. I hear the *tut, tut, tut* of the bathroom fan as the eastern wind blows over the roof, bringing the cold.

You will keep the mind that is dependent on you
in perfect peace, for it is trusting in you. ISAIAH 26:3

Holding

I woke up early this morning
    only to feel the familiar
burn of pain in my wrists. I looked
    out the window
to see the wild oak glowing amber
    in the morning light.
I wondered if her branches ever ached, ever cried
    from holding all those leaves.
Later, I watched my son and his friends climb up
    her limbs, clothes catching
on her swollen knots. I saw how the old oak
    welcomed them even though
I swear I heard her branches moan and bark,
    twigs terrorized under the scuff of boys in sweaty shoes.
This must be how I continue—
    accept, accept.

Don't you know that your body is a temple of the Holy Spirit who is in you, whom you have from God? You are not your own. 1 CORINTHIANS 6:19

A Lesson in Denial

You deny yourself the afternoon snack. You hide the cookies in the pantry so you're not tempted. You eliminate whole categories of food: gluten, dairy, meat, anything whole because you're on a juice fast. (It's what all the celebrities are doing to bounce back three weeks after having a baby, even twins!) You deny yourself the second helping. The first helping. It's your anniversary and you tell the waiter to hold the dressing on the salad. Your hand moves to your abdomen as you tell her you're too full for a piece of your favorite chocolate cake with raspberry drizzle in the shape of the sun. You deny yourself the late summer nights at the swimming pool, the cherry-red two piece with the ruched shoulder straps, the plane tickets to the beach he offers while holding his breath. You tell yourself you prefer pants—even in the middle of the summer under the bright colors of the carnival. Your family is sticky with cotton candy while you and your clean fingers deny the sweat running down your thighs. You deny yourself all of it. You deny that you have not tasted life, you say you are satisfied with this hollow air. But your dark eyes tell the truth: It is hard to want something so little, so much.

Listen, I am telling you a mystery: We will not all fall asleep, but we will all be changed, in a moment, in the twinkling of an eye, at the last trumpet. For the trumpet will sound, and the dead will be raised incorruptible, and we will be changed. 1 CORINTHIANS 15:51-52

Touch Your Face Lightly

I've been thinking about the way you touch your face lightly, fingertips running over the laugh lines and the deep crease on your forehead. There is fear in the touch, shame, and a bit of sadness too. It's how the skin thins on the cheeks and droops around the eyelids and the pores expand, and how you know the six bottles on your counter with antiaging on the label don't stop the truth.

//

I am still somewhere in the middle but the questions started years ago: Injections and fillers and pumping, plumping, tightening, peeling, and *have you thought about it?*

//

We are all just living today wondering if tomorrow we will cross over. When is the moment our currency of youthful beauty is used up and we are worth nothing? When will we be sorry we have lived so long?

//

Maybe, if we cover it, they won't know about the three miscarriages, the sleepless nights, the MRI scans, the rocky marriage, the cherrywood casket. They won't know of our grief, fear, jealousy, and ever-lingering weariness. Let them think we are "other." Let them think there are some of us who are not human. Like a heat mirage in the summer, bend the light around our bodies so they don't know what's real.

//

Her white hair is pulled into a neat bun at the base of her neck. Pearls rest on her mottled throat. Her frail hand waves in the air, the red nail polish glowing in the moonlight: *Oh honey, looks fade. We were not made for eternal youth, we were made for eternity.*

//

Maybe if we band together, we can see the body for the glory it is. Each line a stone in the temple, boldly saying, *We are here, but only for now.*

I have trusted in your faithful love; my heart will rejoice in your deliverance. I will sing to the LORD because he has treated me generously. PSALM 13:5-6

A Note from My Future Self

In your last moments, you will not think of
a smaller pair of pants,
or toned legs for the summer dress,
or a bigger bust after years of nursing.

Instead you will think of how your mother would push
a drawer in with her hip,
the way your husband softly kissed the back
of your knees,
and the rose lips of the child you'd do
anything for.

Your final days will not be filled with thoughts of crow's-feet,
turkey neck,
or sagging skin;

instead you will think of how rare
it was that you had a love that lasted,
how the raindrops beaded
on the roses at your best friend's wedding,
and how your grandmother's blouse
always smelled of gardenia and honey.

You will think of midnights and fire and the way dandelion seeds
float like a river in the air.

You will think of how the sun faithfully moved from east to west
all your years because of His hand,
and the way, even when eclipsed, there was always a glow.

ACT IV

WEAR THE CROWN OF CREATION

We always may be what we might have been.

ADELAIDE ANNE PROCTER, "A LEGEND OF PROVENCE"

THERE ARE NO SMOOTH ROADS in Christianity. Only dips, curves, and potholes the size of a small barn. Over the years, my faith walk has included many high points—seasons when a parade for Jesus marches down the middle of the road—but more often than not, I'm left to dodge the skeletons of apathy, doubt, anger, or confusion sprawled across the pavement. Any one of these seasons might have sent me walking away from Jesus, if not for a resolute and determined belief that He is the one for me—and ultimately, Christ's unending well of grace keeping me at His side.

What I have learned is that faith is often not very easy and certainly not sexy. Instead, faith compels us to step back into the ring as we stagger at the edge of the mat with a pulled hamstring in our right leg. Our faith is often raw and injured, but it keeps fighting. I don't exactly know how it works, but we're both to remain sheltered by the shield of God while also coming out swinging at the enemy. By heavenly design, the life devoted to Jesus is executed through both faith *and* works. We lounge in the Lord's promises and protection while at the same time tightening our shoelaces to run another lap.

Here's the good news: If you have said *yes* to Christ's call, then you are never alone and never without what you need. When you are in Him, you are united to Him—meaning by being His, you have access to everything He has. Christ's deep well of courage, kindness, gentleness, self-control, fortitude (and more!) are also given to you. Which means that no matter where you are or what you're doing, you can draw on His gifts to help you follow Him. Scripture exhorts believers to put off the old ways of the flesh and to put on a new life in Christ—to wear our truest identity: image bearers of God, the crowns of creation.

Each morning, or really each moment, His litany of gifts is available for you. Don't believe the lie that they are for someone else or for another time—they are yours, right now, just begging to be put to holy use in your life. You are loved and known and rooted for by the all-powerful King of the universe, and He has given you the greatest inheritance you can receive: Himself.

You might be battle worn, with dirt under your fingernails and an open cut on your forehead, but you are beautiful to Him. So catch your breath, wipe your sweaty palms on your blue jeans, and get ready to go again. You've got a crown on your head, daughter of God, and you're not going to lose this battle, with Him on your side.

He causes his sun to rise on the evil and the good, and sends rain on the righteous and the unrighteous. MATTHEW 5:45

And Yet

I tell my children that life isn't fair.
They will be kind and someone will hate in reply.
They will work hard with no return for their effort.
They will ask, *Why me?* when the point of life's
arrow is fragile and poisoned toward their heart.
I tell my children: *I know it doesn't make sense.*
We do not always get what we deserve.

I tell my children that life isn't fair.
They will turn their faces away
from the lonely soul in the lunchroom.
They will tell me a lie, because they think,
It is just too complicated. Moments stack,
they will hide and cower, gossip and cheat
—and yet.

The Queen Anne's lace still blooms like a summer
snow in the field behind the house. The stranger
still holds the door when he sees them coming.
The dog still hurtles toward them down the hill,
goofy joy all over his face just because they exist.
As we watch the dog stretch his legs to run,
I tell my children: *I know it doesn't make sense.*
We do not always get what we deserve.

When you come, bring the cloak I left in Troas with Carpus, as well as the scrolls, especially the parchments. 2 TIMOTHY 4:13

Maybe It Is like Touching God

1.
Today it is the fact that I'm sitting on my green velvet couch, a mug of coffee tucked between my outer thigh and the armrest. The dog's head keeps flopping over my lap like he's drugged, his nose pressing down keys on the computer in the middle of my sentences. lj,kljnkljil. I don't delete those because I want to remember.

2.
Some days it's the sound of the piano being plunked by seven-year-old fingers, it's the flickering coals in the fireplace, it's red apples on the counter, it's the nightlight glowing under their door, it's the swale in the pillow where I know he'll sleep next to me tonight.

3.
Have you ever thought to yourself, like I have, *I shouldn't need anything, I have Christ*? But Paul wanted his coat and books so much he wrote to Timothy and asked him to deliver them, and God deemed it should make it into the holy Scriptures—so cannot I ask for coffee and my dog's head resting in my lap?

Paul was so ordinary.

Perhaps ordinary is more sacred than we think.

4.
It's my daughter's body, alive and warm and relaxed in my arms. It's the snow a foot high outside my door, still untouched, and barring some brave animal foraging for food, knowing it is this way for miles and miles and miles. It's them asking, "How many days until my birthday?" 364 days a year. It's the darkness outside while I read my Bible and its insistence that I am loved and part of something so big, so boundless, so utterly beautiful that it keeps me going for another day.

5.
Have you ever thought about how we cannot touch God who is our greatest comfort, but we can touch all these other great things? We can run our hands over our son's soft cheek, the purple knit blanket made by our great-grandmother-in-law, the ceramic mug our father's hands made, even as they shook with Parkinson's. Maybe they are like touching God.

6.
Stop clutching your pearls, you understand what I mean. You cannot tell me you've never thought about Eve pressing her palm to God's? Mary hugging Jesus? What must that have been like? Someday we'll know. For now, we have cheeks and blankets and mugs and this is enough and let's pray we are brave enough to accept them while we do.

For with much wisdom is much sorrow; as knowledge increases, grief increases. ECCLESIASTES 1:18

Primrose

The day I found out my daughter was disabled, the sky blistered blue. And though I cursed it for doing so, the sun still shone—its flaming, happy rays unconcerned for my grief. It is like when the doctor announced it was time for surgery, the friend told everyone the secrets, the pastor preached about how God has a plan. That blasted sun, always shining.

Is there a way to walk into the hard cave of grief and not die? How do you not make a nest of bitter bones on the cold edge of your wounds?

Five years later and here is what I know: In the same way the goldenrod fills the field full of her flowers, spreading further and further every year, the slender soul can expand to absorb the grief. One day you wake up and you find that while you are not completely happy, you are not completely sad either. You discover joy still exists and it is, perhaps, sweeter than before. Friends still make you laugh. Books are still a comfort. Chocolate is still delicious. God is still near. *I'm praying for you* still means something. All of this you now know more deeply than you did before the griefs. You understand what you couldn't before: that rocks and graves make the blooms of the primrose even more beautiful, even more sacred.

Love never ends. 1 CORINTHIANS 13:8

Notes to Self on Marriage

Tell him you like it when he wears a hat. Go to concerts like you are 22. Take at least one spontaneous trip to Paris together. Though it can be like stuffing down a stale cracker, be the first to ask, "Are we okay? I feel like we're off." For goodness' sake, put down your phone. Turn off the TV. Sit on the back porch with a drink in your hand and watch the deer graze in the twilight. Swallow your lecture and offer a prayer instead. Know the landscape of his body, mold, sway, surprise. Be honest about what you need. More words / more listening / more time / more touch. More of him. In a fight, go to bed. Things will look better in the morning. Literally kiss and make up. Tell him you love him, all the time, in every way you know how. But perhaps more difficult, believe him when he says it to you. Occasionally, you will have a moment where you see him from across the room. Maybe he is telling a story. Maybe he is vacuuming. Maybe he is looking at you. When his eyes find yours, press your thumb to your wrist and feel your heartbeat. Remember your life together. Do you see how things have fallen into place? How you have changed for the better? Do you see how he is the one for you and there could be no other? Thank God that he is yours.

You will not grieve like the rest,
who have no hope. 1 THESSALONIANS 4:13

After Death

It was a mostly gentle death,
a small noise, then a soft sigh.
One last breath, and your
soul went home.
Only four months before,
you danced at our wedding
and took your son's
face between your palms
and told him how proud you were.

In the beginning, our grief filled
every room with thick, dragging air.
But then time happened.
While the air did not clear,
it lightened.
Fourteen years later and there
are three new lives
that will never know you as we did.

But we tell them of you.

We tell them of how you loved
the white house on the lake
with its tomato garden
and zinnias, how you liked
milk with a bit
of honey, how you kept
a list of lives to pray for in
your small black notebook.

We tell them of how much you
would love them, of how,
if you were here, you would point
to the trees turning gold
in autumn and say, *Look.*
We tell them of how
you wait for them. That someday,
if they trust Him,
you will take their face
between your palms too.

He comforts us in all our affliction, so that we may be able to comfort those who are in any kind of affliction, through the comfort we ourselves receive from God. 2 CORINTHIANS 1:4

Windfall

I cannot tell you that you
will understand why
everything happens
as it does, and I won't
promise that it
will all make sense
someday. But what
I can offer is that as you
look back on your
life, you will spot
small,
glowing glimmers
of understanding.

There, your heart
was broken and now you
can heal hers.
Here, you faced
a mountain
and now you can
carry him
over his. Over
there, your soul
was softened and now you
can soothe theirs.
It is humanity's best
shared language
on this broken Earth:
selfless love,
and
tenderness.

He is like a tree planted beside flowing streams that bears its fruit in its season, and its leaf does not wither. Whatever he does prospers. PSALM 1:3

The Plum Tree

We are sitting in a circle when K. tells us a story about a plum tree in her backyard. She tells us how every summer it is laden with fruit, so much she can't even gather it all. I imagine the plums lying on the dark grass like a bed of wine-colored stars bleeding into the ground. K. tells us about an afternoon when she is standing by her kitchen sink, staring out the window at the plum tree when a thought occurs:

The tree doesn't keep any of its fruit.

I imagine the tree, plucked and pulled and picked at by strangers' hands. The tree just gives

and gives

and gives.

Freely,

freely,

freely.

It is summer and the plums' red juices drizzle down a child's chin in the yard. It is fall and the plums are scooped out of small glass jam jars and spread thickly over butter and toast. It is winter and the fruit's frozen half-moons are slung into a blender for a smoothie in an attempt at a New Year's resolution. I imagine the fruit given to neighbors, handed out at Christmas, donated to charity auctions, and offered to those with the ache of hunger. On and on it goes—feeding, sustaining, nourishing, yet no one thinks about the tree as they eat the fruit.

But it gives

and gives

and gives.

Freely,

freely,

freely.

I hope it does not scare you when I tell you, like K. did, that the psalms compare the righteous to a tree that bears fruit.

For you are dust, and you will return to dust. GENESIS 3:19

The Dust from Which We Came

Excuse me, God, this might
be overkill, but can I get
an ingredient list on that dust?
I only ask because most days,
I feel like we're all just common
Iowa topsoil, trembling with sweat
and the insatiable needs of the world.

Or maybe we're made of chalk,
the kind that's scraped like a skeleton
off the White Cliffs of Dover
and pummeled into the neighborhood
sidewalk. Honestly, I have wondered
if I'm made of peat, waterlogged and half
decomposed in a backyard bog.

But perhaps you used the fancy stuff,
like kaolin clay, fine as a white
throat and mercifully pure. Or
maybe some of us are from delicately
milled travertine, forged in the ancient
workshops of the false gods.

—Hang on, hang on, these scientists
are saying we're all made of stardust,
supernova building blocks
giving us life from their death.

They think it was all chance but
you and I know there is a created
purpose to this great big world, everything
pointing true north, right to you.

I know the ingredients don't really matter
but I like this last idea best. Celestial
neutron stars collapsing like a fist
under your finger to make a heart pump.
It's unconfirmed, but maybe that's why
these bones of dust and dirt glow
a little when we look at the night-blue sky.
Like calling to like, the Heavens to Earth,
all just begging to be made new by you.

You made him little less than God and crowned him with glory and honor. PSALM 8:5

Queens

My mother says you can always tell how old someone is by their hands. *It's a dead giveaway*, she says. I am in the garden and I catch a glimpse of my hands as they move earth for the meadow sage's roots. They look old. This is the first time I have thought this. Now I stand near the hydrangeas. They have turned green in the caress of hot July nights. They are fuller, sturdier than in June. I picture my mother as she laughs, pulling her short hair out of the visor she wears like a crown. She tells me she loves getting older. *Every year it's less of me and more of Him*, she says. As practice, I make a mental list of all the things I like about getting older.

One: Not caring so much about what other people think of me.

Two: Shamelessly going to bed at 9 p.m.

Three: Owning a citrus juicer.

Four: Having boundaries.

It's going to rain soon, I can smell it.

I add *knowing when it's going to rain* to my list of things I like about older me. My daughter brings me a flower crown made of yellow rockets from the field. She is young and soft and full of life. At her command, I kneel for her to place it on my head—and for a moment I step out of myself. I finally know what it means, I think: My mother, my daughter, me. We are the crowns of creation. I add this new knowledge, this holy effusion of being loved, to my list.

May he give you what your heart desires
and fulfill your whole purpose. PSALM 20:4

Around Three in the Afternoon

I see the start of them at the top of the hill, gold heads moving up and down like a horse's trot, growing bigger and bigger in the powder of the Midwest sky. My children ricochet against their friends, like their shoes are too big, like living pinballs, like they have just been served a drink. When they reach the shade of the honey locust at the end of the drive, they each bend and scoop up a brittle brown pod, ragged thumbnails picking for seeds. As I watch them, all limbs and feet and yellow hair—I need you to know none of this is wasted. Not the monotony or the ideals, the needs or the pain, not the car rides or the floor sweeping, not the drums making the entire house shudder or the purple marker on the table that needs to be wiped clean every day, not the sacrifices the world told me not to make, said would pummel me vacant and flat, said would make me atrophy with want, ravenous for more. They didn't know how laying down my life for my children was where I would feel most full-bodied and grand, each day making me more new and alive than the one before. Sometimes I think about my other life, give it a slight nod across my mind. *This one. I will always choose this one.*

[He] has saved us and called us with a holy calling, not according to our works, but according to his own purpose and grace which was given to us in Christ Jesus before time began. 2 TIMOTHY 1:9, NKJV

Two Mothers

Some days I start the day with low lights and back scratches, letting the dog come cuddle next to the sleepers and nuzzle their faces. I play music and make what they request for breakfast even if it's not what I had planned. I remind them to grab water bottles and my voice sounds like a Disney princess. Did I just sing? I'm not thrown off when the youngest throws a tantrum. I wait it out. I might even laugh. I ask questions in the car and one of us prays. We are mostly on time.

Some days I rip into the room and burst the bright lights on. I rub their backs, but only quickly. I slide the plates onto the counter, whatever was quick, and carry a screaming child to the van while shouting out orders. I sound clipped and a little bit weary. I think of all the things we forgot on the drive and one of us prays. We are mostly on time.

It strikes me then what God tells me is true.
I love you, I love you, I love you. On both days, I love you.
I tear up at that. Yes, because I know I'm not worthy.
But also because there are days when I think I am.

God said, "It is not good that the man should be alone;
I will make him a helper as his partner." GENESIS 2:18, NRSV

Paris

1.
Our luggage was lost somewhere in New York but we didn't care. We stepped off the plane in Paris and bought the necessities: a change of clothes, toothbrushes, two croissants. Then we headed to the Louvre.

2.
We left two jobs, three kids, and a furious sea of change and heartbreak back in the States. It was a spontaneous trip—your work needed you in Europe, the grandparents said *yes*, and off we went.

3.
Sometimes, I think that *love* is too small a word for what we have. Love is not immense enough, enduring enough, sacred enough. We poets demand so much of words and *love* is perhaps the most lacking. I never could have known how it quivers in my mouth. How it rushes onto the page. How it is full of fire and ocean and leaps toward the sun.

4.

On the flight over I looked out the window at the Atlantic. I thought about jellyfish and how they have no heart. How their gossamer bodies seize in the deep dark. They live their whole life without an organ that would let them feel how I feel with you. All that undulating elegance, buoyant and meaningless.

5.

Our suitcases didn't arrive in Paris until our last day. It didn't matter. It was Paris. It was macarons by the Eiffel Tower. It was buying the watercolor in the Montmartre market and shaking the artist's hand. It was you and me, our eyes as big as the world as we took it all in.

6.

And this is the way, isn't it? Nothing going to plan but having everything we need.

Above all, put on love, which is the perfect bond of unity. COLOSSIANS 3:14

Us

We wonder, How will these children ever believe in love?
    Perhaps,
    it will be the way you bring me chocolate
    ice cream in the evenings.
    Or,
how I write on a Saturday morning
    and you make the children pancakes.
    Possibly,
it will be the way you brush your lips
    over mine before work.
    Maybe,
because of how you reach for my hand
    when we argue.
In this fairytale world,
    these children will know what happens
when the princess goes home with her prince.

Lawn care.
Debates on when to get a dog.
Fixing the dryer.
Questions over how much she
is spending on ball gowns.
Dishes. An abundance of dishes.
It's all a bunch of unsexy stuff.
How will these children ever believe in love?
Because of us.
Because of us.

Don't I have the right to do what I want with what is mine? Are you jealous because I'm generous? MATTHEW 20:15

Terrible Math

I tell my children life is full of terrible math.
You will be good and someone will be mean.
You will persevere and it will still fail.
I tell my children: *Bad things happen all the time to good people.*
Soon they will see that the rich get richer as they
  toast champagne
on their yachts, while the poor get poorer as they work three jobs.
They will see the women carrying keys in their knuckles,
the disabled weeping behind the windows,
the people targeted in the parking lot, just for being alive.
But I tell my children: *That is only half the math,*
the other half is just as terrible.
The liar, the cheat, the murderer—
the saint, the holy, the legalist—
  all soaked to the bone in sin,
  all level at the cross,
  all offered new life
  in exchange for open hands and a humble heart.
I tell my children: A good thing has happened for
  undeserving people.

It doesn't make sense, the terrible math of grace.

Love is patient, love is kind. Love does not envy, is not boastful, is not arrogant, is not rude, is not self-seeking, is not irritable, and does not keep a record of wrongs. Love finds no joy in unrighteousness but rejoices in the truth. It bears all things, believes all things, hopes all things, endures all things. 1 CORINTHIANS 13:4-7

When Love Swings by for a Visit

She hustles into the room, pulling her kaftan back on her shoulders. Her lean arms wrap you in a tight hug, holding it for at least 20 seconds longer than you would. Her cheeks are flushed as she touches the baubles on her necklace before kissing you on the forehead. *How are you, sweetheart?* she murmurs while searching your eyes. She has brought you a bouquet of wildflowers from her garden and a loaf of sourdough bread, the kind with ornate swirls and little brown bits on top. Your favorite. Love pulls you to the couch to sit for a chat, but not before whipping out two cups of hot chocolate from her bottomless tote. She is all bright energy and summer glow, a contrast to your winter gloom. You tell her you're sorry for all the ways you've wronged her, but she waves her hand before you can finish, *Water under the bridge, honey.* You sit primly on the couch at first, unsure of it all, but over time, over tears, over truth, you eventually curl up and lean back into the cushions, taking a sip of the cocoa. As its sweet warmth slides down your slick throat, you remember what was forgotten. That even when your world feels like a wound, you are never alone.

When Abram heard that his relative had been taken prisoner, he assembled his 318 trained men, born in his household, and they went in pursuit. GENESIS 14:14

Friendship Is

Raised eyebrows / knowing glances / whispered secrets over coffee mugs. Bringing a meal after a child's surgery / on busy days / just because. Celebrating her new job offer / parental accomplishment / outfit over chips and queso. Crying on the driveway after what he said / an appointment / a phone call. Texting back and forth *I'm coming over in 5!* / medical advice / funny political reels. Telling off a man who's a little too friendly / an unkind Uber driver / her own made-up lies. Reminding her what is true / real / kept in Heaven for her. Giving fashion / marriage / life advice. Saying, *I have no advice at all, but I am here.* / Second / third / fourth / forever chances. Keeping memories / hope/ light / safe.

The water saw you, God. The water saw you;
it trembled. Even the depths shook. PSALM 77:16

God's Favor

It does not matter if you wear cashmere
or cotton, drive a beat-up Ford
or a brand-new Mercedes,
scrape your fork in the mornings
along a gold-flecked china dish or press
it onto a flimsy paper plate: No one can conjure
themselves a better sunset to stretch
across the sky. Even
with all the money in the world,
one cannot force
the milkweed to bloom
on their clock. No matter the riches,
one cannot summon a fawn
from the thicket at will or manifest
a winter snow. These miracles
are the same for all of us, standing here
on the golden shore. No matter who you are,
you can tremble with the waves in this sanctuary
of Earth. You can walk the edge
of the sea with a shiver in your spine.

I follow close to you; your right hand holds on to me. PSALM 63:8

Faith These Days

There are the quiet days of peace. Trust and belief in Him are easy, like the way my children know I will kiss them good night, or my mother knows I will call. There are the muddled days of conflict. A slight war of *do I* or *don't I believe*, like the way I wonder if the number calling is a scam, or if I can trust the salesman. There are the deafening days of abandon. The doubt swells tight around my teeth, like the way I feel alone in my nightmare, or when the doctor utters the diagnosis.

In all of this I continue. Some days I am silent. Some days I scream. I do not always know what I know but one thing is true: I am utterly surrendered to Him. I cannot shake the grip of Heaven. Each day, I grasp for His hand. Each day I find it. A tender miracle.

Rejoice in the Lord always. I will say it again: Rejoice! PHILIPPIANS 4:4

A Short List of the Things I Don't Have

Hips that fit my high school jeans / despair
/ control around carbs / time / false
hope / bitterness / acting skills / a clean
house / perfect punctuality / discipline
for breathwork / bitcoin / a penchant for
boredom / caffeine tolerance / a clean
desktop. Let's see, I also don't have chickens
/ an alarm clock / small hunger / an elusive
laugh / a completed to-do list / a fragile ego
/ a quiet voice / composure when I see an old
friend / an ability to refuse a vacation / small
ideas / small dreams / small thoughts / small
opinions / a small life. What, did you think
this would be a list of things I actually want?
Five years ago I learned to love who He
made me and determined to squeeze every
ounce of goodness out of this one short life—
which means the best thing I have every day
is endless, gluttonous, joy.

My soul, bless the L*ORD, and do not forget all his benefits.* PSALM 103:2

Our Best Life

Remember when they told us we could write the bestseller / get the promotion / start the side hustle / make seven figures / travel the world / create our *best life now*? All we had to do was just follow their lead / take these steps / hit "Subscribe" today / watch that video / comment *Tell me how!* below. Well, we thought about it—almost bought into it—but decided they can keep their *New York Times* bestseller / year-end bonus / upper-level promotion / fancy gold trophy / 20 percent royalties / workplace accolades / 10 percent commissions. Give us all the mundane / the commonplace / the ordinary / the unremarkable. We'll keep our days in the sun, resting our head on the chest of the husband who loves us / the owl footie pajamas in the hallway / the smell of lavender on the front porch / the laughter of friends playing Fishbowl in the living room / the evening walks on the gravel road behind the house. What we're saying is, if it's between hustling to build our fame and being with our people, they can keep the trophy on their shelf / check in their hand / life hacks to themselves. Give us the thousands of forms love takes in the quiet places.

Because right now? We're already living our best life.

Blessed is that servant whom the master finds doing his job when he comes. LUKE 12:43

A Trillion Years

Sometimes I walk in the woods
at night just to hear the quiet.
Tonight the viburnum's blooms glow
like little moons. I pick one to light my way.
I am thinking, as I often do, how not to waste my life.

What will matter in a trillion years?
What do I do today for an eternal deposit?
I sift beyond the pull of retirement,
summer plans, tomorrow's schedule.
Should I be a missionary? Work for my church?
Probably I should give all my money away.
I will do this for you, I whisper
to the Spirit as I walk.

It could be the warm night air,
but I think I feel Him smile.
Do you want to know
what He brings to mind?
Serve your husband.
Patience with the children.
See others the way I do.

All of this effort to conjure
a new life, when all He asks is to conform
the life I am living to Him. I lay
the viburnum's bright bloom on the path.
I walk to my house, my feet light on the limestone steps.
I turn the handle of my back door.
This. This. All of this will matter in a trillion years.

ACT V

BURY IT IN YOUR BONES

My knowledge of that life is small, the eye of faith is dim;
but 'tis enough that Christ knows all, and I shall be with Him.

RICHARD BAXTER, "LORD, IT BELONGS NOT TO MY CARE"

STOP ANYONE ON THE STREET and ask them what Heaven is like, and you'll get any variety of responses, from "Perfect" or "Good" to "Bright" or "Gold." From Michelangelo's famous Sistine Chapel ceiling to chubby babies playing harps in modern-day cartoons, people over the generations have all sorts of ideas about what it will be like. But the truth is, there is a lot we don't know about Heaven. Which is why it can be so hard to look forward to or even trust that it's a real place where believers are headed. But it is real. And we really are headed there.

That changes everything.

When you accept the Crown of Creation in Christ, among the torrent of gifts you lay claim to is the promise of Heaven. Regardless of its seeming ambiguity, the Bible does give us a lot of helpful clues about what Heaven will be like. From Scripture, we know there will be no more sin, pain, or hardship, and our bodies and souls will live with God forever. Heaven won't be boring, like the church service you kept falling asleep to when you were 12. Instead, it will be like the best bite of a summer watermelon, kissing your lover for the first time under the blue-skinned moon, or spotting your child's first steps just before they topple into your arms. It will be so much bliss and beauty your fallen human heart would break if it hadn't already been made new by Him.

While it might still be 15, 30, even 80 years before you walk eternity's shores, this future hope changes everything about your today. When you know you have the promise of an eternal world, you don't have to fear aging or death, or even what happens to you between now and that wonderful, fateful day. While you're not called to be a martyr, if you lay claim to this promise, you can live knowing there is nothing anyone can give you that you don't already have, nor is there anything they can take from you that you truly need.

With Heaven on your heart, your life today becomes less about your own personal résumé and trophies, and more about how you can serve and love others, spreading the good news of this promise to everyone you meet. You don't have to accomplish every goal or dream now, because this life isn't all you have. So bury this truth in your bones, etch it on your heart, and grasp it with a white-knuckle grip as you live today for Him, knowing the promise of Heaven is real, and you're headed there.

*You do not know what tomorrow will bring—
what your life will be! For you are like vapor that
appears for a little while, then vanishes.* JAMES 4:14

After the funeral, we talked.

Remember when we were young
they told us how life is short?
Remember when we spent
afternoons catching snails
in the fields of lily of the valley?
Remember how we prayed God
would turn us into birds so we could
fly with them?

They were right. Life is short. But
when you know how the story ends,
you do not need this life to be long.
Tomorrow is a quivering mystery,
but we are unafraid.
Eternity waits, a soft, quiet charm.
So we continue as we began,
praying to fly.

We were buried with him by baptism into death, in order that, just as Christ was raised from the dead by the glory of the Father, so we too may walk in newness of life. ROMANS 6:4

What I did not know about following God was that it is not all fun and games. When I was young, I loved God the way my brown-eyed dog loves me, hell-bent on never leaving my side. Like the week my church group hiked the Colorado mountains (a real thrill for Iowans), and we sang "I Could Sing of Your Love Forever" around the fire. I was 16 and I wondered if my body might burn up, a firework into the ether. I really could sing of His love forever. My naïveté nearly wept at the thought.

Then two summers later there was the car accident.

The first bits of ash and grief cleaving my heart. He was only 18, all limbs and optimism. We wore pink, his favorite color, to the funeral. Though I didn't know it, that was when the tender shoots of my spiritual honeymoon were clipped. I did not know how over the years my body would empty and cool, and what was between me and my God would be raked through a sieve, pressed for new life. I did not know how my strength and glory would be pulled apart bit by bit until it was myth—until I knew it was always, only His.

"For my thoughts are not your thoughts, and your ways are not my ways." This is the LORD's declaration. "For as heaven is higher than earth, so my ways are higher than your ways, and my thoughts than your thoughts." ISAIAH 55:8-9

Stardust

I always see her at the bakery. Her blue polo
is covered in flour, though I don't think they
let her bake. She shouts my name
over the glass case, the fruit tarts shudder
under her bellow. We have known
each other for years and years and despite
life's opposite tides, we orbit.

She lives in a group home and rides
the bus to work each morning. She
is never late. She tells me the same
story many times in many ways
and I laugh like each time is the first time.
When I met her, I thought we were wood
frogs and ripe oranges—nothing in common.
Mostly I thought I was doing a good
deed, extending a kindness. Oh, benevolent me.

But what of this: We all think we are so different
from each other, moonlight and sea urchins.
But what if we saw beyond
fractures in function, details of divergence?
What if we remembered that we are all
just stardust? Limbs of cosmic dust and old
supernovas, reckoning with this earth,
with each other. What happens when we decide
to speak what is true: *You and me,*
we are the same, to the sheer delight of God?

Look, what if we took the time to rub
the dust from each other's skin?
We would finally see
just how bright we each shine.

By this everyone will know that you are my disciples, if you love one another. JOHN 13:35

Instructions on Motherhood

On Tuesdays, slip love notes in their lunchbox. When you need to leave the house, start preparations twice as soon as you think you should. Put the dandelions they bring you from the yard in a vase by the window. Take note of the small miracles: the rosy cheeks when they come in from the cold, a sock's match, the way they hum up the stairs. Do not google your heavy worries at midnight. Apologize often and press their warm bodies close to your heart. Make it a practice to take them outside and show them the stars. Point out Orion, Tarsus, Gemini, and tell them about the God that made every one. Most things are fixed by honey tea and a blanket. Pray for help often. When in doubt, go outside to give them fresh air and sunlight. Perhaps most importantly, remember motherhood is not a contest. It is not a performance. It is not a measuring stick of your worth. You will not have all the answers, and that is just fine. But what you can have is the courage to live fully in each moment. Don't wait to feel ready or for everything to make sense. Be present. Grow with them. Experience motherhood in every way it is offered. We have so much of them. We have so little of them. It will all be more beautiful than you could ever believe.

For you were called to be free, brothers and sisters; only don't use this freedom as an opportunity for the flesh, but serve one another through love. GALATIANS 5:13

Small Problems

You wonder how you can worry about what
to wear in "times such as these." Times
where someone loses their home to a fire /
a child goes hungry each night / a woman
weeps behind a windshield. How can you
fuss over your phone's broken camera /
whether the bread has GMOs / trying a new
skin-care routine when just down the road,
a friend has lost their job out of the blue?
But may I remind you, there have always
been "times such as these." Times when one
group of friends sings karaoke in a bar while

another gathers around a casket. This is the way of the world. A constellation of light against the dark—your life's joys do not have to be sacrificed for another life's grief. This does not mean you do nothing—of course not—send the check / make a meal / pray to God / serve where you can. Then wake up each morning and drink your coffee, check your email, wash the bedsheets, and take your phone to be fixed. Go to the bar and belt, "Happy Birthday" and mean it. Sing a little off key just because you can.

When Jesus saw his mother and the disciple he loved standing there, he said to his mother, "Woman, here is your son." Then he said to the disciple, "Here is your mother." And from that hour the disciple took her into his home. JOHN 19:26-27

Science tells us a child can carry a piece of their mother's heart inside them for a lifetime.

During pregnancy, a phenomenon called *microchimerism* occurs, where unique genetic cells are transferred between mother and child. In the womb, DNA cells from the child's heart, liver, or another organ cross through the placenta and enter a mother's blood. The cells then search for a place to make a home, essentially colonizing the mother's body: lodging themselves in the brain, the skin, and even the heart.

This process happens from mother to child too. As the child forms during pregnancy, cells from the mother travel through the placenta and embed themselves in her baby—the stamp of the mother fused to her child's body, living on in the lungs, spleen, kidneys, bone marrow, and more. Some cells stay for a time, some last until death.

This process even happens with siblings. Because the mother receives some of each child's DNA, the younger siblings will receive the older siblings' DNA, carrying a mix of their mother's and their siblings' cells in their bodies.

Scientists are trying to figure out why our bodies do this, and evidence suggests there are some startling and extraordinary benefits—like the shared cells helping with healing wounds and building strong immune systems. But I wonder if it is also one way God reminds us we are all connected. We are made for one another and, in a way, by one another. We need each other in the same way we need our heart to beat and our liver to cleanse and our lungs to breathe. We are shaped and formed by the ones we love.

Mothers have long said that having a child is like agreeing to cut open their heart and let it walk outside their body. Now we know: It is more than just a metaphor. We carry them, and they carry us.

Seek to lead a quiet life, to mind your own business, and to work with your own hands, as we commanded you. 1 THESSALONIANS 4:11

Sorry I can't come to the internet right now.

I'm busy slowing down to lie in the sun. Busy
eating popsicles and coloring with chalk with the kids.
I apologize, I'm already overbooked
with trimming the peonies and a water fight,
immediately after
finishing the last book in my favorite series.
You see, I have a scheduling conflict
with the World Wide Web,
I'm wading barefoot in the creek,
laughing at the dog pouncing on crawdads.
I've got to go. I have an appointment to keep.

What's so important, you ask?

I'll be holding my hand
on my child's chest,
just to feel the steady beat of their heart.

Come, my love, let's go to the field; let's spend the night among the henna blossoms. SONG OF SONGS 7:11

Let's Hold Hands

The first time was with friends at a café. We sat
side-by-side. You grabbed my hand
under the table. We didn't look at each other.
But sparks radiated to the sky.
It was everything.

Seventeen years later and we have held hands
thousands of times. Tonight we sit
on the couch and you reach for my hand.
We don't look at each other.
The thrill? Gone. But now?
Comfort. Pleasure. A homecoming.
It is everything.

Two are better than one because they have a good reward for their efforts. For if either falls, his companion can lift him up; but pity the one who falls without another to lift him up. ECCLESIASTES 4:9-10

We Have Come So Far

You hear my joints crack as I walk up the stairs and you ask about my back. We move to talk of when to get surgery on my wrists. You think I should do it now, I want to wait a little longer. We have a seven-year-old who still stretches her arms out to be carried, must be set into a car seat, and needs to be lifted over the slats of a crib at least three times a night. Who will do this when there is a four-month recovery and I am allowed to lift nothing but a pencil? We talk of the house projects we want to do,

the appointments we need to make,
the things we want to learn,
the friends we need to love,
the emails we need to answer,
the causes we want to take up.

The lists are so long we fear we will never reach the end, but we finally understand it is still worth a try. Now I ask you to pull a gray. It is really a white. Coarse. It sticks straight up at my part and the sunlight beacons off it. At the beginning of our love I never would have asked you to do such a thing. We have come so far. *It's hard getting older*, you say with a laugh. I agree, but I am already lost in thought of how it is what I want. Our hands knot and I think about how you, me, this life we've built, it is enough.

Set me as a seal on your heart, as a seal on your arm.
For love is as strong as death. SONG OF SONGS 8:6

What I Want to Remember About Loving You

I want to remember the way you lie on the grass in the summer sun, fingers laced behind your head. The way you pull up your hoodie at the first sign of feeling sick. How you play monsters with our youngest to get her out of a tantrum. I want to remember the way you whistle while flipping pancakes and always think to empty the dehumidifier. I want to remember how you keep your father's memory alive, even with the children who never got to meet him. He would be so proud of you, you know that, right? What I want to remember is what you said in the geneticist's office, about our daughter and disabilities and God. I want to remember all the times you gave up your dreams for ours. How when everything in our life was on fire, you took as much heat as you could. I want to remember when we stood at the lookout over the Julian Alps and I knew I loved you with my whole heart. My eyelashes were fluttering in the wind and I knew I would never forget.

His mouth is sweetness. He is absolutely desirable. This is my love, and this is my friend. SONG OF SOLOMON 5:16

I want to write the world a love poem

but all I can write about is how you brought
a patchwork quilt for us to lay on in the snow.
It was January but you smelled
of wild mint in the summer.
We sat in the field
and you showed me Orion.
I showed you the Seven Sisters.
I knew I loved you then
because of the crease
on your cheek when you smiled,
because we had our entire lives before us,
because I saw you eat your sandwich
with a knife and fork once,
because of how you spoke of your parents,
because I knew you'd move the picture frame
two inches to the left, if I asked.

Look at the birds of the air: they neither sow nor reap nor gather into barns, and yet your heavenly Father feeds them. MATTHEW 6:26, ESV

The world did not implode when we said no.

Instead, it opened like an oyster,
like a tulip in the spring, like curtains
on a stage. Life yawned
before us, pleading, begging, *Fall into me.*
A red carpet unrolled,
the hours sprawled before us.
We clung to the day's curves and planes like barnacles,
hell-bent on swaying to the lullaby of life.
We came to understand that time ticks differently,
away from the routine and rules.
We swam in the river, watched the jay fly, and baked
the red velvet cake, licking the spoons
until our tongues were heavy with sugar.
Listen, do you hear it?
The children, laughing. The husbands,
whispering. The birds, singing.
The thrum of life's goodness
is all around us. Aren't you glad
we had the courage to say no?

Give thanks to the LORD; call on his name; proclaim his deeds among the peoples. Sing to him; sing praise to him; tell about all his wondrous works! 1 CHRONICLES 16:8-9

Things There Are {to Be Grateful For}

There are croissants, naps, tandem bicycles, cinnamon tea, afternoons.

There are paperback books, thin-crust pizza, and breezes through open windows.

There are things you can change—your unhealthy thoughts, your wrong beliefs, your pessimism.

There are sweatpants.

There are people to love.

There are many ways to tell them.

There are thighs that touch and hair that's going gray and lines on your face, and there is the truth that he still believes you're beautiful.

There are grocery deliveries; tiny, sticky, children in your lap; oversized sweatshirts to live in; songs that say everything you can't.

There are ways to forgive the one who hurt you, broke you, scared you.

There are ways to choose not to forget, but to learn and protect and live again.

There are the feelings of being completely irrelevant and unremarkable and unknown when you look up into the night sky and truly, there is a God.

There are a few extra dollars in your leather wallet you can earmark for the homeless person you see on your drive home from work.

There are 1,000 reasons to smile and speak to the intellectually disabled woman at the library even though everyone else is giving her a wide berth.

There are yellow Octobers, joyful birds, childhood memories, pink peonies, and the brown-eyed dog that never leaves your side.

There are rollerblades, molasses cookies, slow mornings, and always, always, always, reasons for hope.

Every good and perfect gift is from above, coming down from the Father of lights, who does not change like shifting shadows. JAMES 1:17

The Best Thing Since Sliced Bread!

Oh, you mean like not having to make dinner / all the kids sleeping in on a summer morning / Parmesan cheese / watching a storm roll in from 20 miles away in the heavy Iowa sky / gifts with tissue paper / reading poetry in the bath / giving someone flowers / second servings / people with crinkles around their eyes / pulling on a pair of tall wool socks / feeling longed for / trampolines / when you know you're being funny / a handmade mug with a little bluebird that appears once you finish your coffee / shaved legs and freshly washed sheets / girls' night out / the way your daughter's friends light up when they see her / paper plates / when someone leaves a room better than they found it / the view from my window / believing the best in others / true forgiveness / the flash of a diamond ring on a new finger / how the worst days can still end in the best ways.

Immediately the father of the boy cried out, "I do believe; help my unbelief!" MARK 9:24

It Happens

It happens in a moment: *This makes no sense. How can I even believe in this stuff? God is as mythical as Zeus, Santa Claus, and that imaginary friend I had in first grade.* You are driving in a car. Sitting on your couch. Getting a drink at Starbucks.

//

It happens in a minute: You tell yourself this is normal. This is part of faith. It's not resistance, it's an element. *I believe, help my unbelief!* Your heart rate rises anyway. That pain you feel in your chest when you are stressed starts. You rub it a little, out of habit.

//

It happens in an hour: You've largely forgotten about it. Distracted by children or texts or whatever. But when you do think about it again, you wonder, *Will it ever go away?* You've been wondering this for years but that doesn't stop you from asking. You think, *What would happen if you left it all behind?* Everything would change. Is that the only reason you stay?

//

It happens in an afternoon: You pick up your Bible and read. You are not totally sure you want to but the habits of grace are a pillar you can wrap your arms around when you are not sure what is real and what is not. You make an investment. You might use it today, but likely it won't be for a few years yet. You know this because right now, you are drawing on five years ago.

//

It happens in a week: Your friend and your husband know that you are struggling again. You told them separately but they respond like they have talked about it. You are frustrated with yourself but they are not with you. You go to church.

//

It happens in a year: You read stories of others who have clung to the cross. *I can do this too.* You talk with people smarter than you. *Yes, yes, this does make sense.* You talk with people who struggle like you. *I am not alone.* You remain because it is so utterly beautiful. You remain because there are moments you know it can't *not* be true. You remain, sometimes, simply because you want to.

//

It happens in a lifetime: You shuffle, day by day, toward the shores of glory. Then one day you see Him. In all His glory, and all His power, and all His majesty, and all His kindness, and all His compassion. All that overshadows all the ways you've failed and doubted and disbelieved and disobeyed. You are overwhelmed, and maybe a little surprised. The Heavens meet your knees and you can hardly bear the look of love on His face. You weep and worship. For the finish. But also for the fight.

Samuel took a stone and set it upright between Mizpah and Shen. He named it Ebenezer, explaining, "The LORD has helped us to this point." 1 SAMUEL 7:12

Remember

You love the world
a little bit too much
and so it breaks your
heart now and then. When
it does, go take
a walk by the sea
and listen to its secrets.
Then, tuck a shell
in your pocket
and return
to the landlocked fields
of corn. When you need it,
lift the briny seashell
to your ear and listen
to the ocean's whisper
again.

Their eyes were opened, and they recognized him. LUKE 24:31

On Thursdays

take care of yourself.
Drink more water. Stop and talk to the plants,
especially the new green shoots. Take a breath
that fills your belly until you could pop it with a pin.
Roll back the bedsheets early. Squeeze
honey in your tea. Eat a crumble filled with summer's
blueberries and lick the fork clean, then later, a carrot.
Stack goodness upon goodness like your daughter's
deck of cards, like your husband's freshly
laundered shirts, like your mother's
brown folding chairs in the garage.
Why Thursdays? I don't know. Pick any day
    and be free.

Because of the LORD's faithful love we do not perish,
for his mercies never end. They are new every morning;
great is your faithfulness! LAMENTATIONS 3:22-23

Coming Soon

In the morning, the dog scratches his ear
with his hind leg while I braid the sun-hair
of my oldest daughter. Out the window a buck
takes a tentative step near the maple tree,
and we watch, like we are the only two
people on the planet who have ever seen one.
Later, my youngest daughter's small hand
presses deep into my rib while her other hand
traces my nose, my cheeks, my eyelashes. While
I listen to her heavy breaths, I think
of school drop-off, the toast browning
in the toaster, the burgundy mums on the porch.
I think of seasons and the way the autumn
wind never blows without bringing change.
There are many winds, but this one, the north one,
is unpredictable air. Is it hope it brings? Love? Want?
Mark this: The gale is heavy with new mercies
and frantic optimism. Today could be
like any other day, but it won't be.

You have said, "Seek my face." My heart says to you,
"Your face, LORD, do I seek." PSALM 27:8, ESV

Thin Places

When you find
one, bury it
in your bones, secure it
like a celestial
suitcase
in your chest.
Let it cling
to the wild thump
of your heart, stretch
your body long.
Then, when life
flings you a strange
creature in an ocean
of rust,
push your hands
into your body, cup
your palms around
the pulsing ebenezer,
and *carry on.*

BENEDICTION

May the LORD *bless you and protect you; may the* LORD *make his face shine on you and be gracious to you; may the* LORD *look with favor on you and give you peace.*

NUMBERS 6:24-26

AS I WRITE THIS, the silk spring skies are turning into the granite blue of summer. Fluffy, homegrown white peonies perfume the air next to me on my kitchen table. Their scent is so strong, I keep wondering if I have a candle burning. These are the days when I find myself looking for any excuse to go outside and check on the flower garden, that perfect in-between time when the spring rains combined with the summer heat make it unhinged and riotous—my favorite state. It is a "hymn of promise" right in my own front yard.

As I leave you, dear friend, I hope you feel you have been seen in some way. Or liberated. Or mended. Or even just settled. Whatever it is, I have prayed for you and for the Lord to do a good work in your soul, in His own way and time. No matter what, know that if you trust Him, He's in the process of changing you toward glory. Remember that no matter how heartbreaking this side of the sky gets—and it always seems to be a bit heartbreaking—you are a daughter of the King, the crown of His Creation. He is always near. He made you, He loves you, and He cares for you. In Him you are bursting with good gifts and an eternal future. Give Him your whole life. You won't regret it.

ACKNOWLEDGMENTS

I **KNOW OF NOWHERE ELSE** to start but by thanking my readers and online community. It was you who pointed out that it was not "lyrical microessays" I loved to write, but instead I had two feet firmly planted in the age-old practice of poetry. It is because of your astute feedback and cheerleading that I wrote this book at all.

Thanks also to my agent, Jenni Burke, who believed in my writing long before she represented me. Thank you to my editors, Kara Leonino, Kaylee Small, and Stephanie Rische, for your thoughtful feedback and desire to make every word the best it can be. I'm forever grateful to my designer, Libby Dykstra, and the whole brilliant team at Tyndale. You took a chance on a poetry book when few in the Christian industry had before, and I'm grateful to partner with you on this project.

I'm so thankful to have a slew of industry and IRL friends and family offering behind-the-scenes support, editing, feedback, and pep talks—Gretchen Saffles, Ashlee Gadd, Amy Gannett, Jordan Paschal, Kaitlin Simmons, Michelle Boshart, Dani Allan, Becca Jensen, Dean and Dianne Jensen, and Vicki and Scott Brace—you are the best cheerleaders a girl could ask for. A deep thanks always goes to Emily Jensen, who is a champion of all my work, helping to challenge and sharpen everything I do. I am the better for it.

And finally, thank you to my husband, Mike, and my three children, Eli, Colette, and Eden. You are my greatest poem of all.

ABOUT THE AUTHOR

LAURA WIFLER is a poet, educator, and bestselling author of books for both adults and children. As former cofounder of the widely loved ministry Risen Motherhood, Laura has long offered Christian women a place to feel seen in the midst of ordinary life. Through her poetry, she is known for giving language to what many women feel but struggle to name—restless aches, delicate hopes, sticky loves, and the invisible tensions of a tender faith.

Over the years, Laura has authored multiple bestselling, award-winning books for children, including *Any Time, Any Place, Any Prayer* and *Like Me*, and is the coauthor of the bestselling book *Risen Motherhood*. She is also the founder of The KidLit Lab, where she helps writers craft captivating children's books and navigate the publishing process. Laura lives in central Iowa with her husband and three children. You can find her on Instagram @laurawifler or at laurawifler.com.

Be kind to yourself,
live well.